First World War
and Army of Occupation
War Diary
France, Belgium and Germany

19 DIVISION
56 Infantry Brigade
Prince of Wales's (North Staffordshire Regiment)
8th Battalion
1 March 1918 - 19 May 1919

WO95/2082/1

The Naval & Military Press Ltd
www.nmarchive.com
Published in association with The National Archives

Published by

The Naval & Military Press Ltd

Unit 10 Ridgewood Industrial Park,

Uckfield, East Sussex,

TN22 5QE England

Tel: +44 (0) 1825 749494

www.naval-military-press.com

www.nmarchive.com

This diary has been reprinted in facsimile from the original. Any imperfections are inevitably reproduced and the quality may fall short of modern type and cartographic standards.

© **Crown Copyright**
Images reproduced by permission of The National Archives, London, England, 2015.

Contents

Document type	Place/Title	Date From	Date To
Heading	WO95/2082-1		
Heading	8th Bn Nth Staffs Feb 1918-May 1919		
War Diary	Nine Wood	01/02/1919	05/02/1919
War Diary	Vallulart Camp	06/02/1919	08/02/1919
War Diary	Trenches	09/02/1919	14/02/1919
War Diary	Barastre	15/02/1919	21/02/1919
War Diary	Bouzincourt	22/02/1919	28/02/1919
Heading	8th Battalion North Stafford Regiment March 1918		
War Diary	Senlis	01/03/1918	06/03/1918
War Diary	Beaulencourt	07/03/1918	20/03/1918
War Diary	Varcous	21/03/1918	28/03/1918
War Diary	Moving	29/03/1918	30/03/1918
War Diary	Wulverghem	31/03/1918	31/03/1918
Heading	1/8th Battalion North Staffordshire Regiment April 1918		
War Diary	Wulverghem	01/04/1918	12/04/1918
War Diary	Kemmel	13/04/1918	19/04/1918
War Diary	Wippenhoek	20/04/1918	20/04/1918
War Diary	Tunnelers Camp	21/04/1918	25/04/1918
War Diary	Ouderdom	26/04/1918	15/05/1918
War Diary	L 14 b 36	16/05/1918	16/05/1918
War Diary	Travelling	17/05/1918	18/05/1918
War Diary	La Chavsee	19/05/1918	28/05/1918
War Diary	Field	29/05/1918	31/05/1918
War Diary	Front Line Mery Premecy	01/06/1918	06/06/1918
War Diary	Support Bois De Courton	07/06/1918	09/06/1918
War Diary	Nippes	10/06/1918	12/06/1918
War Diary	Bligny	13/06/1918	18/06/1918
War Diary	Hautvillers	19/06/1918	19/06/1918
War Diary	Le Mesnil	20/06/1918	20/06/1918
War Diary	Reuves	21/06/1918	30/06/1918
Miscellaneous	Special Notice		
War Diary	Front Line Mery Premecy	01/06/1918	06/06/1918
War Diary	Support Bois De Courton	07/06/1918	09/06/1918
War Diary	Nippes	10/06/1918	12/06/1918
War Diary	Bligny	13/06/1918	18/06/1918
War Diary	Hautvillers	19/06/1918	19/06/1918
War Diary	Le Mesnil	20/06/1918	20/06/1918
War Diary	Reuves	21/06/1918	30/06/1918
War Diary	Brouissy Le Grand	01/07/1918	02/07/1918
War Diary	Avondances	03/07/1918	03/07/1918
War Diary	Aix En Ergny	04/07/1918	12/07/1918
War Diary	Faucquenhem	13/07/1918	05/08/1918
War Diary	Labeuvriere	06/08/1918	06/08/1918
War Diary	Locon	07/08/1918	09/08/1918
War Diary	Trenches Locon Sector	09/08/1918	09/08/1918
War Diary	Annezin	10/08/1918	15/08/1918
War Diary	Trenches	16/08/1918	27/08/1918
War Diary	Support Trenches	28/06/1918	28/06/1918
War Diary	Gonnehem	29/08/1918	04/09/1918
War Diary	Trenches	05/09/1918	15/09/1918

War Diary	Hinges	16/09/1918	21/09/1918
War Diary	Trenches	22/09/1918	02/10/1918
War Diary	Cauchy A La Tour	03/10/1918	04/10/1918
War Diary	Saulty	05/10/1918	06/10/1918
War Diary	Graincourt Area	07/10/1918	09/10/1918
War Diary	Proville	10/10/1918	11/10/1918
War Diary	Cambrai	12/10/1918	16/10/1918
War Diary	Avesnes Les Aubert	17/10/1918	19/10/1918
War Diary	St Aubert	20/10/1918	22/10/1918
War Diary	Cagnocles	23/10/1918	23/10/1918
War Diary	St Aubert	24/10/1918	25/10/1918
War Diary	Cagnocles	26/10/1918	01/11/1918
War Diary	Vendignies Maresches	02/11/1918	04/11/1918
War Diary	Wargnies Le Grand	04/11/1918	05/11/1918
War Diary	La Flamengerie	06/11/1918	06/11/1918
War Diary	Eth	07/11/1918	07/11/1918
War Diary	La Flamengerie	08/11/1918	08/11/1918
War Diary	Taisnieres Bry	09/11/1918	13/11/1918
War Diary	Vendignies	14/11/1918	14/11/1918
War Diary	Rieux	15/11/1918	24/11/1918
War Diary	Cambrai	25/11/1918	28/11/1918
War Diary	Talmas	29/11/1918	30/11/1918
War Diary		02/10/1918	02/10/1918
War Diary		03/10/1918	03/10/1918
War Diary		04/10/1918	04/10/1918
War Diary		05/10/1918	05/10/1918
War Diary		06/10/1918	06/10/1918
War Diary		07/10/1918	07/10/1918
War Diary		08/10/1918	08/10/1918
War Diary		09/10/1918	09/10/1918
War Diary	Talmas	01/12/1918	14/12/1918
War Diary	Montrelet	15/12/1918	23/12/1918
War Diary	Villers L'Hopital	24/12/1918	14/05/1919
War Diary	Le Havre	15/05/1919	15/05/1919
War Diary	Harfleur	16/05/1919	19/05/1919
Miscellaneous	Officer i/c 3rd Echelon Details, Balfour House, Finsbury Pavement, London, E.C.	06/06/1919	06/06/1919

WO 95/2082/1

19TH DIVISION
56TH INFY BDE
19TH DIVISION

8TH BN NTH STAFFS

FEB 1918-MAY 1919

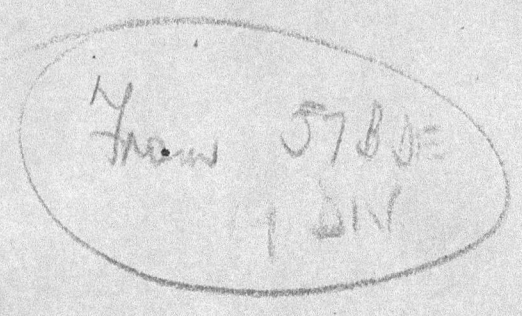
From 57 BDE
19 DIV

19TH DIVISION
56TH INFY BDE
19TH DIVISION

WAR DIARY or INTELLIGENCE SUMMARY

(Erase heading not required.)

Army Form C. 2118.

for February 1918.   8th (S) Bn. North Staff. Regt.   Vol 32

Place	Date	Hour	Summary of Events and Information	Remarks and references to Appendices
NINE WOOD	1st		Trenches. Battn. relieved by 9th Welsh Regt. & proceeded to Intermediate Lu.	
			H.Qrs. RIDGE TRENCH L.31. d.5.2.	
	2		2/Lieut Kendall rejoined from Lewis duty.	
			Batty relieved the 9th K.O.R. Lancs. Regt. as System Batty.	
			"A" Co. KABUL AVENUE	
			"B" KAISER TRENCH	
			"C" KAISER SUPPORT	
			"D" TRENCH L.36.d	
			TRENCH in L.31 & L.32.c	
			H.Qrs. L.32.a.22	
			Relief complete 7pm.	
	3		Trenches. Draft of 43 joined.	
	4		Trenches.	
	5		Trenches. Major Martin gone on leave. Lt. Lord rejoined from course.	
VALLULART CAMP	6		Battn. relieved by Welsh Regt. and went to VALLULART CAMP by Train from TRESCAULT. Arrived Camp about 1 A.M.	
	7		Cleaning up. Battn. leaves 59th Brigade and becomes part of 56d Brigade	

Army Form C. 2118.

WAR DIARY FOR FEBRUARY. 1918.

CONTINUED

INTELLIGENCE SUMMARY.

of 8th (S) Bn. North Stafford Regt.

(Erase heading not required.)

Instructions regarding War Diaries and Intelligence Summaries are contained in F. S. Regs., Part II. and the Staff Manual respectively. Title pages will be prepared in manuscript.

Place	Date	Hour	Summary of Events and Information	Remarks and references to Appendices
VALLULART CAMP	7		SPECIAL ORDER 8th (S) Bn. North Staffordshire Regt. will form tomorrow February 7th 1918 Cadre (6) the long 37th Infantry Brigade and will form part of the 55th Infantry Brigade. The following letter to them has received today by the Commanding Officer from Brigadier General. Asked Cubitt C.V.B. D.S.O. Commanding 37th Infantry Brigade are published for the information of all ranks. "Dear Tonkyn" "Upon your forced and exceedingly sorry to say I am from my command and since your Battalion will be very shortly severed the parting from you and your Battalion is hard. Say on all occasions that it has been your Battalion I can say in this the I appreciate out of all my recognition the officers all bravery and loyal officers who have greatly distinguished themselves on every major Battle in which your Battalion has taken part. I will mention:- 1st attack on 1st June 1917 OBSTAVERNE LINE 2nd attack on 7th June 1917 OOSTAVERNE VILLAGE Mopping up of enemy trenches on 8th June 1917 FORREST FARM FROM AUGUST 5th 1917 SHREWSBURY FORREST on 20th Nov. 1917 Attack on BELGIAN WOOD and SHREWSBURY FORREST In all the above the Battalion did all and more than could be expected of them, and if I am not mistaken you have received more Immediate Awards than any other Battalion in the Brigade.	

Army Form C. 2118.

WAR DIARY
or
INTELLIGENCE SUMMARY.

FOR FEBRUARY 1918

8(3) Bn North Stafford Regt

(Erase heading not required.)

Instructions regarding War Diaries and Intelligence Summaries are contained in F. S. Regs., Part II. and the Staff Manual respectively. Title pages will be prepared in manuscript. Continued

Place	Date	Hour	Summary of Events and Information	Remarks and references to Appendices
VALLULART CAMP	7		To have the Field Show to witness men had won in minutes to fire with recently fired to some the upgrade ready to see at Brigade. Won ill y in very nice was the ill grade won by your Transford in November last. Dash from all the rest if line, and left town shew next up if the upper Battalion was to be the one as other of our was the Brigade	
	8		Sgt Latham & Dligh Heartford awarded Dilgrim Cross & Bronze. Sgtn. Orrin gun to 3 Armed Lion Course. Col Stan Rept Tent Lewis gun Course. D. Co. Col Tent. Strong of Baden etc.	
TRENCHES	9		Battalion relieved 9th Charles Regt in Right trenches of Right sector A Coy Irigaride H Qrs R B. Reserve C Coy Rept tent D Coy Col Tent. Left from YPRES to TRESCAULT Qluez complete 10-10 pm	
	10		Relieved by Train from Trenches. Quiet day	
	11		Trenches Quiet day Draft of 105. Capt Hamond left for 2 months duty in England.	
	12		Trenches Quiet day. Staff Came up	

D. D. & L., London, E.C.
Wt. W1771/M2731 750,000 5/17 Sch. 82 Forms/C2118/14
(A804)

WAR DIARY
INTELLIGENCE SUMMARY.
(Erase heading not required.)

For FEBRUARY 1918 Army Form C. 2118.

Motenvil 9th Bn. Hyd. Staff Off.

Place	Date	Hour	Summary of Events and Information	Remarks and references to Appendices
TRENCHES	13		Trenches quiet day. 2nd Lieut T.W.D Lepine from leave	
	14		Relief of HOOD Battn and proceeded by Railway to ROSQUIGNY SALAMANCA CAMP near BARASTRE arriving abt 6 am & in a.m the 15th	
BARASTRE	15		Cleaning up etc.	
	16		Cleaning and etc.	
	17		Church parade at BARASTRE Huts. Lieut Hood Officer Nursing Report fund	
			Leave recommended (temporary) 2nd Lieut R.J.A. stubbs to Rutalion Capt Bayan Commanding. Lord Denis Stuart Joined to 4th Lancaster Regt.	
	18		2nd Lieut T. Savian from leave. Lort Denis transferred to 4th Lancaster Regt.	
			Capt of 132 Joined. Capt Bryan transferred to 10th R Warwick Regt.	
	19		Training. G.O. inspects A Coy.	
	20		Training. Capt A.H.Bainbridge MC appointed 2nd in Comd. & their Lord and 2 P.B. transferred to 56th DTC. Field Marsh. Training. C.O. inspects B Coy. 2nd Lt Masse returns from Course.	
	21		Route March. Training. C.O. inspects B Coy. Lieutenant returned	
BOUZINCOURT	22		Battalion moved by rail to BOUZINCOURT and camp near PUCHEVILLERS. Le Bord left at 7 pm arrived at ALBERT. Troops in camp near PUCHEVILLERS course at LECHELLE.	

Army Form C. 2118.

WAR DIARY for FEBRUARY 1918

INTELLIGENCE SUMMARY

(Erase heading not required.)

Instructions regarding War Diaries and Intelligence Summaries are contained in F. S. Regs., Part II. and the Staff Manual respectively. Title pages will be prepared in manuscript.

Place	Date	Hour	Summary of Events and Information	Remarks and references to Appendices
BAIZINCOURT	23		Battalion moved to SENLIS by route march. 2/Lieut C.H. HANNES leaves for V.B. to France.	
	24		Church parade in SENLIS 11.a.m.	
	25		Training. AMIENS leave stopped.	
	26		Training. Lieut D.W. Smart from hospital. 4/2nd people leave for Army Infantry School. 2/Lieut Townend goes on leave.	
	27		Training. 2/Lt H.P. Vanner leaves for 3rd Army Infantry School.	
	28		Training.	

19th Division.
56th Infantry Brigade.

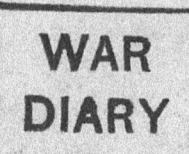

8th BATTALION

NORTH STAFFORD REGIMENT

MARCH 1 9 1 8

Army Form C. 2118.

WAR DIARY
or
INTELLIGENCE SUMMARY.

(Erase heading not required.)

8 N Staffs Regt

Place	Date	Hour	Summary of Events and Information	Remarks and references to Appendices
SENLIS.	1/12/18		Christmas Festivities - sports & dinner to men - 2 Offrs rejoin from Cmd.	
"	2.		Training.	
"	3.		Officers & ors Xmas dinners	
"	4.		Church parade. Stephenson to dinner.	
"	5.		Training.	
"	6.		Remains of the CANAL SECTOR. Training. Inspection of Transport by Brigadier. Return of P.O.W. on R.P.C. work.	
"			Reconnaissance of DOIGNIES for Courts attack. Capt Bird to England (on re duce) – Training	
BEAULENCOURT.	7.		Bn. moves by march & rail to ALMA CAMP. BEAULENCOURT. Entrains AVELUY 9-0 am	
			detrains BAPAUME 10.30 a.m.	
"	8.		Church parade. HERMIES. & Eden to 19 Divn. Training.	
"	9.		Training – GARAGE SCHEME	
"	10.		Church parade. Reconnaissance HAVRINCOURT. Maj Martin rejoins from leave.	
"	11.		Training. 300 men working in Corps Line.	
"	12.		Reconnaissance LOUVERVAL area.	
"	13.		"	
"	14.		"	
"	15.		30 men in Corps Line – remainder training	
"	16.		Training. Gas Schemes.	
"	17.		- 2nd Bowman rejoins from leave	
"	18.		300 men in Corps Line. 2nd Webb gone on leave.	
"	19.		Training.	
"	20.		" 2nd Lindsay rejoins from hospital	

[signature] Lieut-Col.
Commanding 8th (S) Battn North Staffords Regt.

Army Form C. 2118.

WAR DIARY
or
INTELLIGENCE SUMMARY.
(Erase heading not required.)

Instructions regarding War Diaries and Intelligence Summaries are contained in F. S. Regs., Part II. and the Staff Manual respectively. Title pages will be prepared in manuscript.

Place	Date	Hour	Summary of Events and Information	Remarks and references to Appendices
Various	21st	5 am	Enemy attack announced, and order to Stand by received at 5 am. Order to move at 5.30 am.	
		11.40	Order to move to camp 3/4 hour later. On arrival moved country to 6th Div. OPs Camp REMINCOURT. At 11am 5th Div. Ounty alloted DOIGNIES, and at 8 pm 50 O. Rks were up to GN/LA COPSE in support. No definite news had been received during the day and at 11 pm the Bgde was ordered to renew camp at DELSAUX Farm with a view to occupying Green Line behind BEUGNY.	
	22nd		Marching via HAPINCOURT, 160th arrived at rendezvous at 1.30 am and during the night took up a position in the Green Line with 9 Cheshires on right - 25 Div. on left, which was resting on the BAPAUME-CAMBRAI Road. A.B.D. Coys in line & B to L, C Coy in support. Gn/A Copse occupied nominal position in the vicinity of Mill Cross, who had so remained the same throughout the day. During notice time the Enemy was all about the IVLX-MORCHIES Lve, but B wheeled NE of BEUGNY was held by 58 Bgde to our rt. A slight rearrangement of coys took place but the position remained substantially the same. Orders rec'd O.P.M.P was available with 9 Cheshires and 2nd Bge FREMICOURT. The enemy attacks continued beyond outskirts in dug-outs near MORCHIES "BEUGNY" lines with dwns throughout the day, and the troops holding these became front line. Through GREEN lie which by the Enemy had broken. In the course of the afternoon it was reported that the Enemy had entered though on the right towards ROCQUIGNY and the situation became to indicate that warning orders were issued that a withdrawal would be probable. About 11 am enemy attacks Cheshires on our right but with no success. The Enemy had been seen on our immediate front on left. At 2/3, night flank was in the air and orders to withdraw to BAPAUME were received. Enemy were now very close and some of our men were not away to get away. 2/Lt. Carver, Mc Dem, was badly wounded and not to be left.	
	23.			

Commanding 8th (S) Batt. North Staffd Regt.

WAR DIARY or INTELLIGENCE SUMMARY

Army Form C. 2118.

Place	Date	Hour	Summary of Events and Information	Remarks and references to Appendices
Louvres	24		At Sulham was killed, 2/Lt Moore wounded but carries on. The unit claimed was soon out in good order and were soon on very gallantic manner & retiring were met by CO's who kept pressed through RED line at BN CoY which was held by 51 Division and three through positions held by Bn Coys, a line East of BAPAUME where details under Major Marlow (including a strengt of 27 who had joined on the 22nd) had already commenced to consolidate. The line here was held from Q.6.6.) by A,B,C,D Coys, the left company being on the BAPAUME-CAMBRAI Road. The enemy continued to press on the right flank being carried in the air. 16 Coy was compelled to fall back through BAPAUME and eventually took up a new position in support to 56 Bgde of GRENILLERS. The situation during the day has been most unpleasant, no action known the Commanding Officers became Brigade Commander to consolidate again on the spot, and Major Marlow took command of the Bn.	
	25		At 9 am it was decided that the enemy was still moving, and Bn formed a line from W of GRENILLERS to LOUPART WOOD which was held by 51 Div, but this was not known to long and during the morning further withdrawal took place to the ACHIET-L-PETIT-IRLES line (E to railway). Eventually owing to the great numerical superiority of the Enemy and the having of no flanks, we were again compelled to fall back across the railway. The Bn here was split up - H.Q. and some elements of CoY taking up a position along the PUISIEUX-ACHIET Road with 51 Div to 62 Div (who had moved up during the day) on their left. The H Coys under Major Marlow took up a line with 51 Bgde 62 Div	

WAR DIARY
or
INTELLIGENCE SUMMARY.
(Erase heading not required.)

Army Form C. 2118.

Place	Date	Hour	Summary of Events and Information	Remarks and references to Appendices
Ruins	25.		East of Rly at ACHIET-LE-PETIT what was eventually withdrawn to 400 yds West of ACHIET.	
	26.		Bn. H.Q. arrived at midnight to find that the Bn. was to assemble there, and at 3 am some 130 had effected that. The Bn. was to assemble there, and at 9.30 am the advance was carried out along SAILLY Road. when the Enemy was encountered advancing from SOUTH. We were lines along road and fire opened which checked Enemy, but we were compelled to fall back to N.W. of village owing to our artillery shorts. During the day bombardment heavy from HEBUTERNE which was mainly on our trenches — 2nd Bn. Rand. having established a line in S end of the village about 4 p.m. about to join the Enemy made an effort to enter and our line had to fall back to N end of the village. 2nd Lt. Haynes, who had reported from a course was killed here. An Australian officer arrived and took over the line. the O.C. marching to SAILLY-AU-BOIS. The H Coy under Major Martin meanwhile had fallen back to a line East of BUCQUOY, ms. There had orders to rejoin Bn. at HENNESCAMP. They marched from there to FONQUEVILLERS — POMMIER where a halt was made, and then started for SAILLY en route to which place Major Martin at 8 p.m. started a column with O/H.Q. at HEBUTERNE. The O.C. on arrival at SAILLY during the day into the villages on route to FAMECHON arrived, and CO moved off at 2.10 pm hence the march the Divisional Commander advance to Pougeaux and CO has head to 19 Ptr has moved on the position	
	27. 28.			

Commanding 8th (S) Batt. North Staffs Regt.

Army Form C. 2118.

WAR DIARY
or
INTELLIGENCE SUMMARY.

(Erase heading not required.)

Instructions regarding War Diaries and Intelligence Summaries are contained in F. S. Regs., Part II. and the Staff Manual respectively. Title pages will be prepared in manuscript.

Place	Date	Hour	Summary of Events and Information	Remarks and references to Appendices
Moracq	29		Marched on 16 (word) to 2nd Army reserve. C. Coy Coy up to train as loading party at CANDAS Station. Oss left FAMECHON 6 — 11.30 ans arrived CANDAS 4.30. entrained up to form arrived CAESTRE 8 am and proceeded by lorry to LINDENHOEK. C. Coy arrived about 4 p.m.	
	30			
WULVERGHEM	31.		11 Oct took over MESSINES Sector as Oss, made up of 16 WULVERGHEM support to 51 Ords. B Coy given Corps Line in posts forward of MESSINES. Relay Complete 9.30 p.m. [signature]	
		10h.	Many by the Battalion records, viz some alarms, when he has been reports 16 Figures about 10 28. 1 am off the and lost.	

56th Brigade.
19th Division.

1/8th BATTALION

NORTH STAFFORDSHIRE REGIMENT

APRIL 1918.

8(S) Bn. North Staffs. Regiment

WAR DIARY

for Month 1918

INTELLIGENCE SUMMARY.

(Erase heading not required.)

Army Form C. 2118.

Place	Date 1918	Hour	Summary of Events and Information	Remarks and references to Appendices
MULVERGHEM	April 1st		Cleaning up	
	2		Cleaning up	
	3		Draft of 80 O.R. joined. Training.	
	4		Regimental classes commenced - training	
	5		Draft of 125 O.R. joined. Working parties - Some of bringing on sick of Brigade in present operations.	
	6		Working parties.	
	7		Working parties. 2nd Lt Nash returned from leave. 2nd Lt Rutter to Division.	
	8		Brigade Sports commenced under Major Moxon - attended by ... 2nd Lt Blomming attached to 8th Suffolk for R.S.	
	9		Orders for relief of 8th Division in right sector which was to take over that night were cancelled at 12 noon and Battn. ordered to stand by ready to move at short notice. Later news was received that the enemy had turned thorough on the LAVENTIE front and 19th Divn were ordered concentrate in RAVENSBURG area. Major Hanton went to Lowson Heath and later the B.O. was instructed to command 55th Brigade and Major Hanton was ordered to command the Battn.	

8(c) Bn North Stafford Regiment

WAR DIARY
INTELLIGENCE SUMMARY
for April 1918 continued

(Erase heading not required.)

Army Form C. 2118.

Place	Date	Hour	Summary of Events and Information	Remarks and references to Appendices
WULVERGHEM	10		Operation order went issued at 3 a.m. for the Bn to move up to Atherstone Camp at	
		5.15 a.m	but news was received through that the Brigade were attacking on our front and Battn was ordered to stand by awaiting further orders. About 8.30 a.m.	
			51st Brigade issued orders for two of our companies to move up at once and occupy the front & support lines in front of MESSINES, and A & B Coys moved off to do so. B. front line - A Support.	
			The enemy however had by this time overrun the Eastern edge of MESSINES and these two Companies after making a very good attempt to get through the village were obliged to adopt a line running N through the HOSPICE in U.2.A. to C.D.4.6.1.	
			Meantime Battn had moved up to occupy O.G. front line in T.6.b and Battn HQrs was established in dug out at T.6.c.1.6. Situation on flanks was obscure and about 2 p.m. C & D Coys moved up into line and position from R.6.L. meeting roughly C.A.B.D. with centre on rd at HOSPICE which Battalion remained the same throughout the night.	
			D Coy S.A. Brigade counter attacked MESSINES at about 7 p.m. with success but was unable to hold on and withdrew to our line	

Army Form C. 2118.

8th (S) Bn. North Stafford Regt. **WAR DIARY** for April 1918 continued

INTELLIGENCE SUMMARY

(Erase heading not required.)

Place	Date	Hour	Summary of Events and Information	Remarks and references to Appendices
WULVERGHEM	10th		On this day the Batty. suffered heavy casualties. Casts. Muir & 2/Lt Cresswell were killed & Lt Deane wounded & about 150 O.R. killed & wounded.	
"	11th		During the morning enemy attacked 25th Division to our right and made a heavy barrage on our front and many attempts from right of MESSINES. Hai was repulsed. The pressure on the right became increasing and orders were received that a withdrawal was contemplated. Orders were received to consolidate at SPY FARM. Where 8 tm withdrawal commenced from the right and elements of A.C. & B Coys commenced to withdraw through WULVERGHEM and this was stopped and line re-taken. At 11 p.m. definite orders were received and word passed that line was to commence to withdraw at 1 a.m. 12th and Batty. were to make for SPY FARM. Capt. Oakes was wounded during the evening. Commencing at 1 a.m. Bn. moved via WULVERGHEM, DAYLIGHT CORNER to LINDENHOEK receiving en route the orders that they were to hold the Army Line N. of	
"	12		LINDENHOEK and at SPY FARM and eventually casualties were no [?]	

A6945 Wt. W11422/M1160 350,000 12/16 D.D.& L. Forms/C/2118/14.

Army Form C. 2118.

WAR DIARY
INTELLIGENCE SUMMARY

of 8(S) Bn Hon. Artal Regt. for April 1918 Continued

(Erase heading not required.)

Place	Date	Hour	Summary of Events and Information	Remarks and references to Appendices
WULVERGHEN	12		R Boundary LINDENHOEK - WYTSCHAETE Road at N.27 d 2.8 the bearing the hostile Loopers in line from R&L	
			L Boundary KEMMEL - WYTSCHAETE Road at N.21 d 7.3 with all Coys in line from R&L	
			C.D.A.B which dispositions remained throughout the day	
			57th Bgde on right and Composite Bn of 58th Brigade on left towards VIERSTRAAT. Battn H Qrs at N.27 a 2.9 Companies were commanded by	
			A Coy 2Lt Parr - B Coy 2Lt Farvis C Coy 2Lt Stevenson - D Coy 2Lt Jones.	
			In the afternoon 2Lt Edwards joined the Battn and was posted to B Coy	
			Later the C.O. took command of the Bn. and Major Morton went back to 56th Brigade transport during the day had moved to WESTOUTRE-BERTHEN Road and 56th BRIGADE to WESTOUTRE.	
KEMMEL	13		Bn. H.Qrs to N.20 D 55.50 Enemy were attacking during morning at NEUVE EGLISE	
			and later situation here was apparently restored. KEMMEL Hill defences were being	
			held by elements of 49th Divn. Wind: H on heavy firing was directed at	
			WYTSCHAETE but no infantry action took place, and the remainder of the day	
			and night passed quietly.	
			Transport had now moved to rear RENINGHELST and surplus personnel to LA MOTTE CAPPEL	49

Army Form C. 2118.

8th (S) Bn. Hereford Stafford Regt. WAR DIARY FOR April 1918 Continued
or
INTELLIGENCE SUMMARY.
(Erase heading not required.)

Place	Date	Hour	Summary of Events and Information	Remarks and references to Appendices
KEMMEL	13th		Where Colonel Snow took command of the 19th Brit: Wing.	
"	14th		Again this morning enemy appearers continued in the vicinity of NEUVE EGLISE and the situation here was so uncertain that the Battn were ordered to form a new line if necessary in N.32 & 33 facing S.E. or to stand up to the position at NEUVE EGLISE. Ultimately at 11.15 p.m. all units of the 57th Brigade except 10th R. Warwick Regt. & 9th N. Staff were ordered to withdraw and reorganize in ROSSIGNOL CAMP.	
"	15th		Major Martin came up to command the K.S.L.I. who had rallied in ROSSIGNOL CAMP. Reported that enemy had attacked with success at SHELL FARM. At 10-30 a.m. orders were received that the Battn was to man the KEMMEL defences from N.21 & 31 to N.27 & 4 and this was done in moving D.Coy to the extreme right. Second S. and C. Coys were staying to their right and half of SE. B. Coy were brought from the 2nd in and filling the gap left by the withdrawal of the Order of Coys from now from R to L. — D C B A. KEMMEL HILL was fairly heavily shelled during the afternoon. Lu'ish Heath was recommenced to entrench 56th Brigade and were withdrawn at BUTTERFLY FARM	

Army Form C. 2118.

8th (S.) Bn. North Stafford Regt. WAR DIARY for April 1918.

INTELLIGENCE SUMMARY.

(Erase heading not required.)

Instructions regarding War Diaries and Intelligence Summaries are contained in F.S. Regs., Part II. and the Staff Manual respectively. Title pages will be prepared in manuscript.

Place	Date	Hour	Summary of Events and Information	Remarks and references to Appendices
KEMMEL	16th		Orders were received at 1.30 a.m. that 10th Bn. would withdraw from present front line and that there to remain the METEREN - KEMMEL line. C.D. Coy. Frontage remained roughly the same except that C Coy. took over another two hundred yds. of REGENT Trench running tuet and then joined with the 10th S. War batt. who continued the line towards SPANBROKMOLEN. B Coy. moved two platoons to support D and the remaining two platoons to B Coy. together with two platoons to support D. A heavy barrage opened on the hill. (WYTCHAETE) about 5 a.m. and later it was found that the enemy had pushed our line from the ridge and eventually he reached SPANBROKMOLEN CRATER. All day a heavy barrage was kept up on KEMMEL HILL and from 3 p.m. onwards our right (D) Coy. was heavily shelled. About 7 p.m. the 9th Sik. and French troops counter attacked WYTCHAETE. A Coy. of S.A. reached 0.19 Central but the French were not able to retake SPANBROKMOLEN CRATER. The enemy during the evening started forward on D Coy front to a position in T.2.d. the heavy shelling all day caused about 40 Casualties in the Battalion and 2 Lt. Jarvis was wounded and injured	

Army Form C. 2118.

8(C) Bn North Stafford Regt WAR DIARY for April 1918

INTELLIGENCE SUMMARY. Continued

(Erase heading not required.)

Place	Date	Hour	Summary of Events and Information	Remarks and references to Appendices
KEMMEL	16		The night was quiet	
"	17		KEMMEL HILL was again very heavily shelled from early intervals. About 11 a.m. O.C "D" Coy reported enemy on the ridge in N.33 a.1.6. Our artillery hard shots in this direction for a few times during the day. 2nd Lt Lindsey in conjunction with 51st T.M.B. did some good shooting here during the morning and altogether the enemy seems to have suffered a good many casualties here. French troops - 2nd Battn 2nd Regt were put in on various places together with and in support of our companies. No change took place in our dispositions during the day. Enemy shelling was repeated and very all day and about 25 casualties were inflicted. The Brigade carried out another operation at SPANBROKMOLEN in the morning but no news of the results came through.	
"	18		The night was quiet but again in the early morning the heavy bombardment recommenced. At dawn there was a fairly heavy mist, and the Bosh on our right sent up the S.O.S. No action occurred on our front.	

A6945 Wt: W11422/M1160 350,000 12/16 D. D. & L. Forms/C./2118/14.

Army Form C. 2118.

8(S) Bn North Stafford Regt. for April 1918

WAR DIARY
INTELLIGENCE SUMMARY. Continued
(Erase heading not required.)

Place	Date	Hour	Summary of Events and Information	Remarks and references to Appendices
KEMMEL	18		Bn. 1 a.m. Wiring Party were requested that the Bn. would be relieved today by the 28th Frenchmen who would take over the responsibility of the defences from 12 NOON. Shelling continued throughout the day. Unable to actual [K]place and the enemy apparently with drew his line. About 10.00 p.m. Bn. moved DAYLIGHT CORNER. He branch of the Seaforth Returning Party did not materialize up to midnight.	
"	19		Enquiries were made & messages sent out to find where the relief was. At 1 a.m. the 11.22 Regiment declared themselves satisfied and C Coy whom they relieved (and with whom they had been in the Front [line]) and went WEST of LINDENHOEK, the relief was carried out by the 30th Regt. who with with -drew villages and who had the Sections for the our position until 5 a.m. Meanwhile A + B Coys who were on the Miss Regt Front (EAST OF LINDENHOEK) were ordered to withdraw when the relief complete was carried through at 5.20 a.m. The Battalion proceeded via BUTTERFLY FARM - CANADA CORNER - WESTOUTRE to WIPPENHOEK where they were entrained on Light trains & Buscees	
WIPPENHOEK	20		Further personal and draft of 5 Officers, 1 Warrant Officer & Battalion reported	

Army Form C. 2118.

8th (S) Bn North Stafford Regt. WAR DIARY 1918 April 1918 continued

INTELLIGENCE SUMMARY.

(Erase heading not required.)

Instructions regarding War Diaries and Intelligence Summaries are contained in F. S. Regs., Part II. and the Staff Manual respectively. Title pages will be prepared in manuscript.

Place	Date	Hour	Summary of Events and Information	Remarks and references to Appendices
WIPPENHOEK	20		Lt Jarvis-Jones & 2 Lt Majors, Wood, Husband, Simons, Sprague & the from L	
			Wearing up and Kit inspection	
TUNNELERS CAMP	21		Bn marched off at 9 am and marched to bank near PROVEN recommitting	
			was done and tents were erected for sleeping in about ½ the Battn - remainder in huts	
	22		Training & Manor	
	23		Training	
	24		Training 2 Lt Wilson joined	
	25		Training	
		10.30 pm	Orders were received to move to BUSSEBOOM and twenty bullets were erected by 148th Brigade.	
		11.40 am	The Battn moved off in rear of the children. Transport remained in camp	
OUDERDOM	26	3 am	Arrived at OUDERDOM & the Battn was billeted in sheds	
		4 pm	Received orders to move and took up a position N. of OUDERDOM. Bn H.Qr. being at Shell-Lock at G 23. b. 9.4. Situation very quiet during the day. Scouts and Runners	
			to move at short notice. Transport moved to camp opposite to TUNNELERS CAMP	
	27		2nd Lt Patee C. Inf. recommitted Juts which would probably have to be taken up by the Battn	

8th (S) Bn. North Staff Regt. WAR DIARY for April 1918 Continued

WAR DIARY or INTELLIGENCE SUMMARY.
(Erase heading not required.)

Place	Date	Hour	Summary of Events and Information	Remarks and references to Appendices
OUDERDOM	28		Very quiet during the day. Heavy bombardment started about 7.3.m. and continued all night.	
			One Officer sent to Brigade H Qrs to ascertain instructions as the situation was very obscure	
	29		During the day gas shells fell in our area causing a few casualties. Bombardment continued until noon, when it was reported that the enemy had attacked but had been beaten back leaving our line intact.	
			Surplus personnel moved to camps in K.1.C.	
	30		Situation very quiet until evening when OUDERDOM was very heavily shelled. Received warning order that the 19th Divn would relieve the 21st Divn in the line from S. edge of RIDGE WOOD to FRENCH FARM I.27.a. (Sheet 28 N.W.) 2 Lts Lowe, W. Tomb, 2 Lt Glover, Machine Parchment Thompson Tuck Moore joined	

J.C.....
Lieut Colonel
Commanding 8th (S.) Battn. North Stafford Regt.

Army Form C. 2118.

WAR DIARY or INTELLIGENCE SUMMARY

(Erase heading not required.)

8th North Staffs. Regt.

Vol 35

Place	Date May 1918	Hour	Summary of Events and Information	Remarks and references to Appendices
OUDERDOM	1		Battalion in Support at OUDERDOM. 2/Lt. Spraggins wounded. Following Officers arrived Transport Lines and proceeded to join Bn. in support at OUDERDOM. 2/Lt. Brockhurst & 2/Lt. Green, I.R, 2/Lt. Machin, S.H., Lieut Moore J.L. & 2/Lt. Thornton P.L. 2/Lt. Absalom Gore rejoined from Hospital and proceeded to join Bn. in support.	
	2		2/Lt. Myers from 5th T.M.B. Bn. moved to Support lines near DICKEBUSH. Received personnel at L.1.0.3.6. and closes under Sale 9.0.1000.	
	3,4,5		Bn. in Support near DICKEBUSH ditto ditto ditto ditto ditto ditto	
	6			
	7		Bn. relieved and recons of ditto in Camp at L.14.t.3.6	
	7a		Lecture up up stops etc.	
	8		ditto	
	9		ditto	
	10		Church parade held being Ascension Day. Surplus personnel moved to Transport Lines at L.I.C.3.u. Bn proceeded to LEFT SUB SECTOR of 19th Sub SECTOR (in relief of 9th Welsh Regiment) Major J.H. Morris commanding. Letter of congratulations received from General Rotillie commanding 2nd S.S. Corp.	
	11		Surplus personnel moved to Transport Lines at L.1.3.u	
	12		Bn. in LEFT SUB SECTOR 2/Lt. Edin R.S. wounded & remained on duty.	
	13		Bn relieved and returned to Camp at L.14.t.3.6. O Coy being transported at transport lines L.1.3.t.	
	14		316th of Bn. N.C.O.'s O.R. French Sub. Lieut. attached received orders to command Major Marshi went to command 9th Cheshire Regt.	
	15		Cleaning up etc. Enemy shelled vicinity of Camp with H.E. Shells causing 14 Casualties. Training etc.	

Army Form C. 2118.

WAR DIARY for MAY 1918
INTELLIGENCE SUMMARY. 8th North Stafford Regt.

(Erase heading not required.)

Instructions regarding War Diaries and Intelligence Summaries are contained in F.S. Regs. Part II, and the Staff Manual respectively. Title pages will be prepared in manuscript.

Place	Date 1918	Hour	Summary of Events and Information	Remarks and references to Appendices
	MAY			
L.14 & 24	16		Training etc.	
Travelling	17		Bn. entrained at 11.50 a.m. and travelled via CALAIS etc. First stop at NOYELLES	
do	18		Travelling all day via PONTOISE – CHATEAU THIERRY & EPERNAY and detrained at VITRY LE VILLE at midnight	
LA CHAUSEE	19		Arrived in billets at 4 a.m.	
do	20		Training	
do	21		do	
do	22		do	
do	23		do	
do	24		do	
do	25		do	
do	26		Bn. at Sports on canal. H.Q. Rgt won cup. 2nd Lieut Grant T. joined.	
do	27		Training	
do	28		Bn. entrained at midnight for unknown destination. Surplus personnel remained in Billets	
Field	29		Bn. arrived at Epoyes N. of CHAMBRECY at about 12 noon. Received instructions to move up position on ridge N. of NESLE-PRENSEY. Situation very quiet during the night	
	30		The enemy attacked and we had to fall back slightly. The following officers were wounded. Capt. J.O. Jones 2/Lt T. Bennett, 2/Lt Young, Lt Foster. Lt Col Derigate DSO	
	31		Major Martin from the Bn. to 1/7 C. Command. Situation very quiet during the rifles. Surplus transport remained at MONCETZ from 24th to 31st on division	J.C. Cast [illegible]

A6945 Wt. W14422/M1160 35,000 12/16 D.D. & L. Forms/C/2118/14.   Commanding 8th (S.) Battn. North Staff...

Army Form C. 2118.

8TH N. STAFFORD REGT WAR DIARY for June 1918

INTELLIGENCE SUMMARY
(Erase heading not required.)

Instructions regarding War Diaries and Intelligence Summaries are contained in F. S. Regs., Part II. and the Staff Manual respectively. Title pages will be prepared in manuscript.

56/19

Place	Date	Hour	Summary of Events and Information	Remarks and references to Appendices
	1918			
FRONT LINE MERN PRENEGNY	1 June		Situation very quiet on our front all through the day.	
	2		Aeroplanes and Artillery very active on both sides. 2 huns Brethwirk & Mostow wounded.	
	3		Nothing to report during the day	
	4		Great artillery activity on both sides otherwise nothing of importance happened. Surplus personnel moved to VERTUS by lorry with transport wing.	
	5		Shelled very heavily at intervals during the day. Had to reorganise Bn Headquarters.	
	6		Attacked by enemy at dawn. Bn greatly distinguished itself by maintaining its positions when very heavy MG and machine gun fire with high trench mortars and co-operating in successful counter-attack. Major Naster, Lts Lipton & Newman Lt. WARREN 2nd Lieuts Channing & Edle wounded. 2nd Lieut W.B. Randall died of wounds.	
			Bn relieved by the 150th composite Brigade and proceeded to BOIS DE COURTON to re-organise	
SUPPORT BOIS DE COURTON	7		Lt. Col. S.D. Rochdale DSO took command of the Battalion	
	8		On Resting	
	9		Drafts joined into 5th Comrade Battalion & 8th North Staffs becoming No 3 Company. Surplus personnel returned to MORAIN LE PETIT. Bn moved to Vicinity of NIDGES in immediate support to front line	

(A9475) Wt W2358/P360 600,000 12/17 D. D. & L. Sch. 52a. Forms/C2118/15.

Army Form C. 2118.

8TH N. STAFFORD REGT. WAR DIARY for June 1918.

INTELLIGENCE SUMMARY.
(Erase heading not required.)

Instructions regarding War Diaries and Intelligence Summaries are contained in F. S. Regs., Part II. and the Staff Manual respectively. Title pages will be prepared in manuscript.

Place	Date 1918	Hour	Summary of Events and Information	Remarks and references to Appendices
NIPPES	June 10		Bn. in enemy attack, support to front line	
	11		ditto	
	12		Surplus personnel formed Transport lines at HAUTVILLERS. Bn. took over night out-sector of 19th Bn's front.	
BLIGNY	13		Quiet day. Lieut Baxan 2/Lieut Nurses awarded 2nd Bar to M.C. r Persons joined. Letter of thanks received from General Tasker, Lately C.M.G. D.S.O. on his taken quitting Command of 57 Brigade	
	14		quiet day	
	15		ditto	
	16		ditto	
	17		ditto	
	18		quiet day. Bn. relieved by Italians marched to HAUTVILLERS and were accommodated in huts together with surplus personnel.	
HAUTVILLERS	19		Bn. rested.	
LE MESNIL	20		Bn. moved by march route to LE MESNIL. 56th Brigade awarded CROIX de GUERRE.	
REUVES	21		Bn. moved by lorry to REUVES area and accommodated in billets. Letter of congratulation to 56th Brigade - copy attached - from General commanding 5th French Army	

Army Form C. 2118.

8TH N. STAFFORD REGT WAR DIARY for June 1918.

INTELLIGENCE SUMMARY.

(Erase heading not required.)

Place	Date 1918	Hour	Summary of Events and Information	Remarks and references to Appendices
REUVES	June 22		Bn. cleaning up, inspections re. Capt. R.P. Emerson (R.A.M.C.) awarded D.S.O. 2/Lt (A/capt) H. Stocoman, 2/Lt M.S. Randall, 2/Lt (A/capt) K.O. Jano awarded MILITARY CROSS. 60220 Sgt. Manorium A Coy awarded D.C.M. 26626 Pte Topham D. Coy awarded MILITARY MEDAL. Major/Martin M.C. rejoined from Hospital.	
	23		Bn. Church Parade. Shops. Football Match - Bn. Teams - v. 5th CHASSEURS. Lieut A.E. Hore & No. 40659 L/cpl Jackson mentioned for conspicuous conduct in operations of June 6/8. Extract from order No 60 from General Commanding 5th French Army - attached - Training etc. Shops. No 8907 R.Q.M.S. Jones awarded MERITORIOUS SERVICE MEDAL.	
	24		Major/Martin M.C., 2/Lt (A/capt) A.E. Hore & No 40659 L/cpl Jackson awarded CROIX DE GUERRE with Star. Draft of 1 officer (2nd Lt Yeats) & 195 O.Rs joined Bn.	
	25		Training etc.	
	26		Bn. route march. Shops.	
	27		Training etc. Draft of 27 O.Rs joined to return football match played with the 5th 06 CHASSEURS	
	28		Training etc. Capt. L.W. Redden see li 59th Brigade	
	29		Inter Battn. Horse Show Inspection of Transport by Divisional Commander.	
	30		Bn. moved by route march to BROUSSY LE GRAND	

E.R.M.
Lieut. Colonel.
Commanding 8th (S) Battn. North Stafford Regt

Copy.

SPECIAL NOTICE.

Extract from Order No. 60. by the General Commanding the 5th French Army.

The 56th Brigade under the command of Brigadier General R. M. Heath.

On the 6th June 1918, charged with the defense of the important position of the mountain of BLIGNY, they maintained their positions for many hours against the attacks of an enemy superior in numbers and who had almost surrounded them.

Obliged by the last attack to give ground, they counter-attacked immediately. This attempt being checked, a new counter-attack, led with magnificent dash by the Battalion in reserve, threw the enemy from the BLIGNY mountain, took 30 prisoners, and re-established entirely the line which was then maintained in spite of violent bombardment.

(Signed) Pelie. Commander 5th Army.

Copy.

SPECIAL NOTICE

Extract from Order No. 604 by the General Commanding 5th French Army Corps.

Captain A.E. Gore - 8th (S.) Bn. North Staffordshire Regiment.

This officer shewed remarkable bravery during the operations on the 6th June 1918 at the mountain of BLIGNY. During a difficult situation he rallied the men of his Battalion, and organised a counter-attack which retook all the ground temporary lost.
He afterwards took command of his Battalion successfully when his Colonel was wounded.

No. 42659 L/Cpl. Jackson F. "D" Coy. 8th (S) Bn. North Staffordshire Regt.

During the operations of the 6th June 1918, this N.C.O shewed great courage and coolness. After the temporary loss of the Mountain of BLIGNY, which exposed the flank of his battalion, and created a very critical situation, he quickly rallied his men, formed a defensive flank and continuously encouraged his men.

8TH N. STAFFORD REGT. WAR DIARY for June 1918

INTELLIGENCE SUMMARY

(Erase heading not required.)

Army Form C. 2118.

Place	Date 1918	Hour	Summary of Events and Information	Remarks and references to Appendices
FRONT LINE NEST PRENEUSE	1st (cont)		Situation very quiet on our front all through the day.	
	2		Aeroplanes and Artillery very active on both sides. 2nd Lieut. Broadhurst & Matthews wounded.	
	3		Nothing to report during the day.	
	4		Great activity on both sides otherwise nothing of consequence happened.	
	5		Surplus personnel moved to VERTUS by lorry with Battalion War Hd Quarters. Shelled very heavily at intervals during the day. Had to remove Bn Head quarters	
	6		Attacked by enemy at dawn. Bn greatly distinguished itself by maintaining its positions under very heavy shell and machine gun fire with both flanks exposed and co-operating in successful counter attack. Major Harker & Capt H. Freeman Lt Withington, 2nd Lieuts Horning & Este and 2nd Lieut M.J. Randall died of wounds.	
SUPPORT BOIS DE COURTON	7		Bn relieved by the 150th Composite Brigade and proceeded to BOIS DE COURTON to re-organise. Lt Col. 20. Kentish D.S.O took command of the Battalion.	
	8		Bn resting	
	9		Brigade moved into the 56th Composite Battalion. 8th N. Staffs becoming the 3 Company Composite Battalion. Bn moved to MORAIN ST PETIT Bn moved to vicinity of NUISY in immediate support to front line	

Army Form C. 2118.

Instructions regarding War Diaries and Intelligence
Summaries are contained in F. S. Regs., Part II,
and the Staff Manual respectively. Title pages
will be prepared in manuscript.

8th N. Stafford Regt. WAR DIARY for June 1918.

or INTELLIGENCE SUMMARY.
(Erase heading not required.)

Place	Date	Hour	Summary of Events and Information	Remarks and references to Appendices
	2		[illegible] Church Service at 6.30 held at the [illegible]	
	5		[illegible]	
	6		[illegible]	
BLIGNY	7		[illegible]	
			[illegible]	
	11		[illegible]	
	12		[illegible]	
	13		[illegible]	
	14		[illegible]	
	19		[illegible]	
HAUTVILLERS	20		[illegible]	
LE MENIL	21		[illegible]	
REUVE	21		[illegible]	

(A9475) Wt W2358/P360 600,000 12/17 D. D. & L. Sch. 52a. Forms/C2118/15.

8TH N. STAFFORD REGT. WAR DIARY for June 1918.

Army Form C. 2118.

Instructions regarding War Diaries and Intelligence Summaries are contained in F. S. Regs., Part II. and the Staff Manual respectively. Title pages will be prepared in manuscript.

INTELLIGENCE SUMMARY
(Erase heading not required.)

Place	Date	Hour	Summary of Events and Information	Remarks and references to Appendices
REVEG	June 22		Bn. clearing up after move. Capt. A.F. Emerson (RAMC) awarded D.S.O.	
			2/Lt E(temp) A.B. Gower N.S.R. Randall 1/6 (attached) T.O. attached Military Cross	
			49098 Cpl. Harrison A Coy awarded D.C.M. 265 Sgt. T. Hand D Coy awarded Military Medal	
	23		Morning Service by Revd Martin A/C. required from Hospital.	
			Bn. Church Parade. Later Inter Platoon Football match Bn Team - 1/5 3rd Chasseurs	
			Capt. A.E. Gower & 10 Other Ranks Inspection for conspicuous conduct in operation	
	24		of June 6/18. Word from orders notice for General Commanding 3 Division - attached	
			Training etc. A top RAMS found	
			Administration Reg. 2/Lt (temp) A.B. Gower showing Lt Fletcher orders to O.C.M. of GUARDS visited Bn	
	25		Bath of 1 Officer 2/O. Ranks, & 198 OR. joined Bn.	
			Training etc.	
	26		Bn. route march. Shops.	
	27		Training etc. Bath of 2/7 O.R. Parade a review Football match played with the 3rd (2 Chasseurs)	
	28		Training the. Bath of O.R. Parade us 12 Sgt parade	
	29		Inter Battn Associated Athletics of Transport by Divisional Commander etc.	
	30		Bn. entrained by trails and to BROUSSY LE GRAND	

.... Lieut. Colonel
Commanding 8th (S.) Battn. North Stafford Regt

Army Form C. 2118.

8TH N. Stafford Regt. WAR DIARY for July 1918

INTELLIGENCE SUMMARY

(Erase heading not required.)

Instructions regarding War Diaries and Intelligence Summaries are contained in F. S. Regs., Part II. and the Staff Manual respectively. Title pages will be prepared in manuscript.

Place	Date 1918	Hour	Summary of Events and Information	Remarks and references to Appendices
BROUSSY LE GRAND	July 1		Battalion moved by route march to FERE CHAMPENOISE and entrained for MARESQUEL in the British Zone.	
	2		In train journey.	
	3		Arrived MARESQUEL Station about 11 am. Bn. moved by march route to AVONDANCES having breakfast en route.	
AVONDANCES	4			
AIX EN ERGNY	5		Bn. moved by march route to AIX EN ERGNY.	
	6		Training. Draft of 120 O.R. joined Bn. Major Larter M.C. & Capt. Stone promoted to Crosses at ST. VALERY. The following officers joined :— 2/Lt R.D. Trevor-Jones, R. Alcock, 2/Lt L. Oldland & W. Oxley.	2/Lts & O.R.'s 9 Pm
	7		Church parade.	
	8		Training. Capt. B.J. Colls rejoined Bn. Lieut Col. H. Bainbridge M.C. 2/Lt W.J. Brockhurst awarded Military Cross. On his being placed at disposal of Bn. whilst arrayed officer I.	
	9		Training.	
	10		Training. 2 Officers 1.50 O.R. proceeded by rail for sea bathing at WIMEREUX nr. BOULOGNE.	
	11		Bn. route march. 2/Lts C.J. Simons and W.J. Brockhurst awarded Military Cross R.S.M. H Tennis awarded D.C.M. W.Q.M.S. Scott awarded meritorious service medal.	
	12		Training. Bn. moved by march route to VERCHOCQ CHATEAU and then entrained for FAUQUENHEM, arriving about 3 p.m. being accommodated in billets.	
FAUQUENHEM	13		8 O.R. proceeded to join 19th divisional mounted detachment.	

Army Form C. 2118.

8TH N. STAFFORD REGT WAR DIARY for July 1918

INTELLIGENCE SUMMARY

(Erase heading not required.)

Place	Date 1918	Hour	Summary of Events and Information	Remarks and references to Appendices
FAUCQUENHEM	July 13		2/Lt. J. Wright joined Bn. & posted to D. Coy. Church parade.	
	14		Draft of 31 O.Rs. joined Bn.	
	15		Training etc. 2/Lt. C. Wright finished from D. Coy & H. Coy. and taken over duties of Signalling Officer. 2/Lt. Parsons (to be D. Coy). Major Martin M.C. & Capt. Cope returned from leave. 2/Lt. Graney to Carlisle joined *Bn.	
	16		Training etc. 2/Lt. Graham 2/Lt. Graney & Carlisle joined *Bn.	
	17		Draft of 11 O.R. joined Bn. 2/Lt. Roberts transferred from D. Coy to H. Coy. Bn. route march. Takes over duties of Intelligence Officer. Recruiting party for round men	
	18		Training. Classes. Reconnoitring party for forward area	
	19		Training. L.tarns etc. Staff of 3" O.R. Consist: Party reconnoitred forward digestion to Brigade H.Sn. for inspection area. Reconnoitring party for forward area Visit of Divisional Follies	
	20		Training etc. Reconnaissance of the line.	
	21		Church parade. Draft of 29 O.Rs. joined Bn. Capt Bell M.C. right draft of 2/Lt. G.O. Howard, 1/6. Capel, & St. Madden (Gord. Bn.	
	22		Brigade scheme. 2/Lt. G.O. Howard, 1/6. Capel, F.G. Wyrd, (Gor.) Sharri, Capt. F.H. Carver (from Austin P)	
	23		Training. Classes & competitions. 2.O.R. joined Bn. Capt. Bell M.C. takes over duties of Adjutant and 2/Lt. G.O. Howard the duties of assistant adjutant. Football match.	
	24		Training. Classes etc. Tests of Entrenchment Tools.	
	25		Training. Classes. Transport Competitions. 2/Lt. Parsons proceeds on depot command	

Army Form C. 2118.

8TH N. Stafford Regt. WAR DIARY for July 1918.

INTELLIGENCE SUMMARY.

(Erase heading not required.)

Instructions regarding War Diaries and Intelligence Summaries are contained in F.S. Regs., Part II. and the Staff Manual respectively. Title pages will be prepared in manuscript.

Place	Date 1918	Hour	Summary of Events and Information	Remarks and references to Appendices
FAUCQUENHEM	July 25		21st Divisional Signal School. Brown Drills. Reconnaissance. Last all important Brigade Transport Competition won by 8th North Staff Regt.	
	26		Training. Warm re Batt: Minor Repairs from 5 9th Brigade.	
	27		Training. Warm re Sports. 2/Lts Jarvis attended Reconnaissance by Mr Le Brun Barrett at CAMP 15. 2/B 7/5 2/Lt Myers goes to 16th & T.M.B.	
	28		Platoon Marching Competition. Church Parade. 4/G Lemon proceeds to VIIIth Corps school Report much attended by	
	29		afternoon & evening. Br. Lupi.	
	30		A day thus showing the Bn. Cup. Training. Classes re Football Match. Training. Bn. inspected by Brit. R.O.C. Lt Trevor-Roper Proceeds to [mi?] 2nd N. Staff (Siege) Left. Visit of Savannah Miller.	
	31		Training. Classes as Brigade Platoon Competition.	

[Signature] Lieut. Colonel,
Commanding 8th (S.) Batta. North Stafford. Regt.

8TH N. STAFFORD REGT. WAR DIARY for August 1916.

INTELLIGENCE SUMMARY

Army Form C. 2118.

Instructions regarding War Diaries and Intelligence Summaries are contained in F.S. Regs., Part II. and the Staff Manual respectively. Title pages will be prepared in manuscript.

Place	Date 1916	Hour	Summary of Events and Information	Remarks and references to Appendices
FAUQUENHEM	Aug 1st		Training. Classes. Bn. ordered to send B Coy as Brige	
	2		B.O.I. instruction to Corps.	
	3		Training & transport now formed (provisional). One of Demand Lists	
	4		Lewis Bombers. 2nd Lieuts returned from Gas Course	
	5		Training. Bath parades by Coys to Estaminet – Les	
LABRUNSIÈRE	6		Bn. marched to entraining point B.N.6.2.5 entrained Pepin in Reserve to brigade D.2.a.0.0.1 where the road running into Robecq	
			On relieved the 1/8th R. Lyrs in front line Logan Sector Composition of Lsyt as follows: Right A to work (Bdy H.Q. N.74 K.M.5.) D Coy Centre (C. Aug 30.3.9 Left B Coy left (Bdy H.Q. N.74 K.M.5) 20.0.0 Rifles and Patrol were sent out and no enemy encountered. Our casualties of enemy M.G. auto pounder	
LOCON	7			
			wounded.	
	8		Patrolling both days & nights – casualties this day 2nd Lt Dawson Killed Officer (2Lt Richmond) & 2.O.R. killed. 5 O.R. wounded. Laying wire beyond our line Patrol now went out to locate F. Guston some M.G. rounds went over the wire then Lewis brought fire dispersed on	
	9			

8TH N. STAFFORD REGT — WAR DIARY for August 1918

Army Form C. 2118.

Place	Date	Hour	Summary of Events and Information	Remarks and references to Appendices
TRENCHES LOOS SECTOR	9		8 O.R. wounded during the day. One shell on road and one shell on our front line. 1 Officer (Capt Jarvis) & 12 O.R. wounded.	
	10		Usual day of operations. 2 O.R. wounded. 5 O.R. sick.	
ANNEZIN	11		Bn relieved by 1/4 Cheshires & sent back into Bn Training. Capt Davenport returned to Bn.	
	12		Bn completed in billets. 1 to 8 a.m. M.O. & 2/Lt McDermott went to Bn.	
	13		Training	
	14		Training	
	15		Lecture. 2nd Lts Longshaw, Jones to Bn. Lieut H. Stone rejoined Bn on leave.	
	16		Lecture & Baths. 2nd Lt Hewitt went to Hosp.	
	17		Training. Draft Pte — 30 Canada Corps ??? joined Bn.	
TRENCHES	18		Bn relieved 9th Ches Regt in SUPPORT	
	19		"	
	20		A Coy moved forward and occupied EDINBURGH TRENCH. Relieved by 9th Cheshires on advance. A Coy in relief moved as advanced guard. 9 O.R. wounded. 1/6 North, 1st South. Left 20/hill.Wounds to long field of fire in front of RAT. To hill not found on...	

8TH N. STAFFORD REGT.

WAR DIARY or INTELLIGENCE SUMMARY

For August 1918 (continued)

Army Form C. 2118.

Place	Date	Hour	Summary of Events and Information	Remarks and references to Appendices
TRENCHES	21		Bn. relieved 9 Cheshires in OUTPOST LINE.	
	22		Patrol of 1 O.R. and 2 O.R's. left our lines at 7.45 pm on reaching a point 20 yards from enemy N/9 post the patrol came under heavy gun and M.G. fire. The enemy in strength. Patrol returned to our lines emerging no casualties.	
	23	7.30pm	Pte Edwards killed during enemy artillery fire on our outpost line by gunshot wound. T.M's sent out a patrol to establish touch. Got out about 100 yds to the rear of the enemy's wire and encountered M.G. & sniper fire. Returned about 20 yds from enemy lines. 12 Gloucestershire A.T. Bn. sandpits turned at CHOCQUES.	
	24	4.45pm	Bn. H.Q. X.16. 2.B. was heavily shelled with 5.9 for fifteen minutes.	
		2.30pm	Bn. H.Q. moved to Orchard dugout on road & X.13 w.10 to B 69 m and 9.5.6.5. Bn. LEICESTERS 300 yds to left of 20 Brigade line.	
	25	4.01pm	A Coy (in support of reinforcements) relieved Bn. A Coy of M/9 Sherwood Foresters Bn. 2. B Coy in support w.o. DAWN. BANK.	
	26		Capt. S.B. Grew in charge. 2nd Lts Whitehouse & Preece through Bn. in support Toy. Arthur in B. G.H.Q. 75.	
	27		Bn - "Valley" pass to trosser dyke. Bn improved trenches, dugouts, move they & raw cut electric road	

Army Form C. 2118.

WAR DIARY or INTELLIGENCE SUMMARY.

8th N. Stafford Regt

(Erase heading not required.)

Instructions regarding War Diaries and Intelligence Summaries are contained in F. S. Regs., Part II. and the Staff Manual respectively. Title pages will be prepared in manuscript.

Place	Date	Hour	Summary of Events and Information	Remarks and references to Appendices
SUPPORT TRENCH.	28		[illegible handwritten entries]	
	29			
COMMECHEM.	30			
	31			

....
Lieut. Colonel.
Commanding 8th (S.) Battn. North Stafford. Regt.

8 N Stafford R
951 39

WAR DIARY / INTELLIGENCE SUMMARY

Army Form C.2118.

Place	Date	Hour	Summary of Events and Information	Remarks and references to Appendices
GONNEHEM	1/9/18		"B" attended Brigade Church Parade at the conclusion of which the Army Commander presented Medal Ribbons to officers & O.Rs of the Brigade. — The following of this Bn were the recipients of ribbons. MILITARY CROSS 2/Lieut E.E. Simmons. DISTINGUISHED CONDUCT MEDAL No 12884 C.S.M Tamoina H, No 67410 Sgt Mamarow J. MILITARY MEDAL No 42706 Sgt Cook G.H, 18745 Sgt Aston S, 38508 Sgt Truslove T, 15839 Cpl Saker H, 48762 Cpl Martin A.W, 23280 Cpl Handley B, 40223 L/Cpl Handy J, 19031 L/Cpl Whitaker S, 241102 Pte Fletcher J, 141145 Pte Brooks J.T, 1119 Pte Royles G, 18993 Pte House G, 40786 L/Cpl Horsley F.	
GONNEHEM	"		Draft of 3 O.R. joined Bn	
"	2/9/18		Training, cleaning, etc	
			Warning orders received. "B" to be in readiness to move on 2 hours from 5 am 3rd inst.	
			Lt Col Daykins (D.S.O) rejoined Bn". Capt Gore returned from Course.	
"	3/9/18		Training, etc. Capt Pedder & Capt Daws rejoined from leave. Training cancelled.	
"	4/9/18		Operation Orders for relief by 5/6 Bgde on night of 4/5 cancelled.	
			Warning orders received for Bgde to relieve 59th Bgde in the Line on night of 5/6.	
			Lt Hunter & Lt Ekington rejoined Bn	
TRENCHES	5/9/18		"B" entrained at GONNEHEM, detrained at LOISNE, where tea was provided, afterwards marched to RICHBOURG & relieved 1/5 Leicesters (46th Division) in out-posts line. Relief complete about 12.	

Army Form C. 2118.

WAR DIARY
or
INTELLIGENCE SUMMARY.
(Erase heading not required.)

Instructions regarding War Diaries and Intelligence Summaries are contained in F.S. Regs., Part II. and the Staff Manual respectively. Title pages will be prepared in manuscript.

Place	Date	Hour	Summary of Events and Information	Remarks and references to Appendices
TRENCHES	5/9/18		Front Coys "A" on right, "B" on left. Enemy line crossed at British front line. Support being "C" on right "B" on left. Supports being the British Reserve Line. 3" H.Q's on route "B".	
"			B" being right B" of 5th ARMY, where connecting up with 1st ARMY on our right. B" on right being 1/5th Kings Liverpool Regt (55th Division)	
"	6/9/18		Quiet day. Patrols pushed out at night and reported Bank showing 02n German front line with Machine Guns.	
"	7/9/18		Brage of 11 Officers + 330 O.R's joined B" (2Lts R Bare, & Reeves, R & Harris & F Kent). "A"+"D" Coys sent out strong patrols and established posts in Old German front line. Enemy Machine Guns having impaired any withdrawal. — 2/Lt Snyder was on Gas Course.	
"	8/9/18		2/Lt Hadsworth (A Coy) met with a strong hostile and Enemy saw aware sent at 1 pm and was attacked a post about 200 yards S.E of DU BOIS FARM during of outpost line enemy snipers were very active. "D" Coy immediately indicated forward posts in conjunction with "A" Coy. — "A" + "D" support platoons (2 each) moved	
6 BOIS TRENCH (old German Front Line).			"A" support platoon heavily attacked with S.A.I.	
			(4 killed 16 wounded) Capt Emmerson reported nipress fires down. P.F.	

(19175) W1 W3536/P340 500,000 12/7 D.D.&L. Sch.5m. Forms/C2118/20.

WAR DIARY
INTELLIGENCE SUMMARY

Army Form C. 2118.

Place	Date	Hour	Summary of Events and Information	Remarks and references to Appendices
TRENCHES	9/9/18		Night of 8/9th 2/Lt Summers + 3 O.R. (D Coy) patrolled area in front of SHEPHERDS REDOUBT. Information asked for by Brigade obtained by this patrol. 2/Lt S. MYFAN attached to 81st R.E.'s — Boche snipers + M.G's very active 2/Lt 2.0 Downs "A" Coy wheres by snipers in vicinity of forward positions. From this statement met & wounded were the previous 2/Lt the West wounded.	
"	10/9/18		Major Hatri gave an resume. Night of 9/10th "C" + "B" relieved "A" + "D" respectively in forward positions. "C" + "B" Coy harassed by snipers immoderately. 7.30 am Capt Downs "C" Coy Killers over command of near of Rt left's forward post. — Lt Bellington takes over command of "C" for the day. — At about arrive from Transport lines & takes over command of "C" Coy. Patrol of "C" Coy under 2/Lt Tate patrolled Boche positions in front & good information was obtained. 2/Lt Summers "D" Coy was wounded by M.G bullet.	
"	11/9/18		Lt Bellington "C" Coy with 10 O.R's in conjunction with 5th South Lancs made several futile attempts to establish a post at LA TOULOTTE FARM. "B" Coy continuously sent out patrols which invariably came under MG fire of the enemy. Two sects of platoon of "B" Coy under Old German Front Line attacked by "PIP SQUEAKS"	
"	12/9/18		At 10 am "C" Coy again attempted to establish a post at LA TOULOTTE FARM but owing	

Army Form C. 2118.

WAR DIARY
~~INTELLIGENCE SUMMARY.~~
(Erase heading not required.)

Instructions regarding War Diaries and Intelligence Summaries are contained in F. S. Regs., Part II. and the Staff Manual respectively. Title pages will be prepared in manuscript.

Place	Date	Hour	Summary of Events and Information	Remarks and references to Appendices
TRENCHES	12/9/18		In the early morning the garrison of the sniper's ramparts was "D" Coy. BOARS HEAD shelled with gas shells at midnight. —— At 2 p.m. enemy TRENCH MORTARS shelled SHEPHERDS REDOUBT, our forward posts and the ramparts being reasonably untouched. —— "B" Coy established at SHEPHERDS REDOUBT.	
"	13/9/18		About 5.30 a.m. about 30 shells (5.9") fell mainly at B.8.d.4.2. Transport's journey at 2 Sentry Groups 300 yards from ESSARS was shelled about 7 a.m. for 3/4 of an hour, causing 2 men return journey. In the afternoon 9.2" Howitzers shelled SHEPHERDS REDOUBT. Our forward posts were again withdrawn for the purpose. When the shelling had ceased "B" Coy had extreme difficulty in re-establishing them back, owing to the activity of enemy snipers which were difficult to locate. Night 13/14th Bn relieved by 9th Cheshire Rgt. true of relief "B" H.Q. and Draft by Kings Road. Draft of 190 R.s joined. 2/Lt Mac Livingstone. Lt R.L. & Lts "E.A."	
	14/9/18		L'EPINETTE & RICHEBOURG ST VAAST occupied.	
	15/9/18		Transport horses shelled at 7 a.m. for about ½ hour. Coys improved positions & commenced salvage work. Barrage was thin down in day. 2/Lt Capel goes on course after Survey returns from same.	
HINGES	16/9/18		Bn relieved by 8th Gloucesters (57th Bgde) marched to HINGES arriving about 9.30 p.m.	①

(Ag.123) Wt W3455/P396 600,000 10/17 D. D. & L. Sch. 819. Forms/C.2118/13.

Army Form C. 2118.

WAR DIARY
or
INTELLIGENCE SUMMARY.
(Erase heading not required.)

Instructions regarding War Diaries and Intelligence
Summaries are contained in F. S. Regs., Part II.
and the Staff Manual respectively. Title pages
will be prepared in manuscript.

Place	Date	Hour	Summary of Events and Information	Remarks and references to Appendices
HINGES	16/9/18		"B" Coy detected reveille with 4 vs. "B" accommodated in Billets + Bivouacs at HINGES.	
"	17/9/18		Cleaning up etc. "B" inspected in the afternoon by C.O.	
"	18/9/18		Training, classes etc. visit of Divisional Band. 2/Lt Simmons goes on L.G. Course.	
"			2 W.O.'s + 5 N.C.O.'s to Base for exchange + tour of duty in U.K. for 6 months.	
"	19/9/18		Training etc.	
"	20/9/18		Training etc. Lt. Potts goes on course.	
"	21/9/18		Training etc.	
TRENCHES	22/9/18		"B" left HINGES at 3 pm + proceeded by rail from AVELETTE BRIDGE to relieve 9th Welsh Regt (58th Bgde) in the right front sub-section of the left Brigade Front of Corps. Front:- "A" right "D" left:- Support "C" right. Relief complete 11 pm. Draw of Coys during day. 2nd Lieut's to hospital sick. 2nd Lieut Back wounded. Capt Plowelly "B" left. 2nd Lieut Back 2nd Lieut Marks + Capel rejoined from courses, returned from Hospital. 2nd Lieut Marks + Capel rejoined from courses.	
"	23/9/18		Quiet day.	
"	24/9/18		Quiet day. Enemy paraded in of "D" Coys posts, but was observed off with casualties.	

Army Form C. 2118.

WAR DIARY
of
INTELLIGENCE SUMMARY.
(Erase heading not required.)

Instructions regarding War Diaries and Intelligence Summaries are contained in F. S. Regs., Part II. and the Staff Manual respectively. Title pages will be prepared in manuscript.

Place	Date	Hour	Summary of Events and Information	Remarks and references to Appendices
TRENCHES	24/9/18		Divs. observation / Mellas. 7 Wounded	
"	25/9/18		Quiet day. Arrangts to get Lewis workings to Amat for relief. Arrival 2/Lt Spencer-Evans to SANDY TRENCH	
"	26/9/18		Quiet day. B⁰ relieved by 9th Cheshire Rgt. Relief complete 11 pm.	
"	27/9/18		A Coy, D Coy, HK ammn dump & Retaliation Orders of Coys – Right to Left. "C" "A" "D" "B"	
"	28/9/18		Baths & working parties. 2nd Lt. Crowe returns from leave. do. — do. — 2nd Lt L.C. Smith joins Bn.	
"	29/9/18		Working parties.	
"	30/9/18		Working parties. B⁰ relieves 1/1st Kings Shropshire Regt. 20 Infantry in Jefferson Section. Orders of Coys – Front – C right – B. left – Supports A right – D left. Relief complete. 8 am 1 hour.	

[Signature] Lieut. Colonel
Commanding 8th (S) Batt. North Stafford Regt.

3/1 N. Stafford Regt. WAR DIARY for October 1918

INTELLIGENCE SUMMARY

Place	Date	Hour	Summary of Events and Information	Remarks and references to Appendices
TRENCHES	Oct.1		Quiet day. Information received from air reports and other sources that the enemy was withdrawing.	
	2		Patrols by B/Coy along railway but not established beyond the line. By 2 p.m. AUBERS RIDGE had been crossed and not in touch on W. WELCH REGIMENT (23rd Brigade) of AUBERS. Drawn wire received by 2/Lt WARDEN & 2/Lt GOODALL but evidently wounded. 2/Lt Roberts returned from Roll Coy. Snipers patrols marched from ESSARS to CAUCHY A la TOUR arriving 4 p.m. 2/Lt Ball wounded 11/1/5 pm. Bn marched to CALONNE RICOUART and entrained 2 a.m. 5th Capt R ALUM (S.M. in comd)	
CAUCHY A LA TOUR	3		for CAUCHY A LA TOUR arriving at 1 p.m.	
	4		Bn cleaning up.	
SAULTY	5		for SAULTY arriving at 2 a.m. 5th.	
	6		Bn cleaning up etc.	
			do 2 movers prepared from tonight.	
GRAINCOURT AREA	7		Church Parade. Bn entrained 2 h.m. & arrived 6.37 pm at E 23 a (GRAINCOURT AREA) & accomodated in bivouacs & bone pieces from PARIS Camp. 2/Lt Roberts from on leave.	
	8		Cleaning up Camp.	
	9		Training etc. Bn left our Camp from 3 occupation at E 29 d. (GRAINCOURT AREA) 2/Lt Warren from on leave. Proville arriving about 7 pm.	
PROVILLE	10		Bn marched to PROVILLE arriving about 7 pm. Capt R Alum and Bn Hdqrs + 2 O.R. Capt Watson to F. in command from leave	

Army Form C. 2118.

WAR DIARY for October 1918

6th N. Stafford Regt

INTELLIGENCE SUMMARY

(Erase heading not required.)

Instructions regarding War Diaries and Intelligence Summaries are contained in F. S. Regs, Part II. and the Staff Manual respectively. Title pages will be prepared in manuscript.

Place	Date 1918	Hour	Summary of Events and Information	Remarks and references to Appendices
PROVILLE	Oct. 11		Bn. cleaning up PROVILLE AREA & burying dead. (British & Germans.) 2/Lt Landrey to England as candidate for R.A.T.	
CAMBRAI	12		Training. Major Martin M.C. rejoined from leave. Bn. took over Billets from 3rd Worcesters at CAMBRAI.	
	13		Nonte Cleaning up	
	14		C.O.'s Church Parade. Training re. 7th Division. 7.15 Mcrfs & Tails rejoined from France. One Officer & 7 O.R. reported sick to hospital.	
	15		Bn. carried out Tactical scheme re organisation. 2/Lt Porter rejoined from 3rd Army Reserve. 2nd i/c W.O. & 56th T.M. Battery. 2/3rd Lt unwell. 2 L. Rdr Sqd.	
	16		Training Rt. R.C. Church Parade. – Baths. Lt Pate proceeds on 3 mths leave	
AVESNES LES AUBERT	17		6th L. Rdrs Regt. Bn. moved by march route across country. Recnd (Recce) terrain en route to AVESNES LES AUBERT. Adv stop 3 pm. 2/Lt Young joins from leave.	
	18		H.Q. Officers to Brussels. Training re terrain. 2/Lt Wylie rejoined from leave. Orders received to return to reserve support in notable move in notice.	
	19		Training to France. Bn. moved to St AUBERT. Various personnel remained at AVESNES LES AUBERT	
ST AUBERT	20		Bn. marched to Cavallico (civilians). Roadside O.M. Stores & supplies. Personnel moved to St AUBERT. Bn. came back this area until 6 St AUBERT. During the night the enemy shelled H.V. transport and many of Cavallico & O.R. killed & 2 wounded	
	21		Cleaning up & Training of Billets. 9/6 NE Cleaning 9 Battn front	

Army Form C. 2118.

WAR DIARY 8th Hunts Cyclist Regt. for October 1918

Instructions regarding War Diaries and Intelligence Summaries are contained in F. S. Regs., Part II. and the Staff Manual respectively. Title pages will be prepared in manuscript.

INTELLIGENCE SUMMARY.
(Erase heading not required.)

Place	Date	Hour	Summary of Events and Information	Remarks and references to Appendices
ST. AUBERT CAGNOCLES	Oct. 22		Training &c. Capt B.C. Hanson rejoined Bn.	
	23		Bn moved to CAGNOCLES preceding Division. Taken over in trucks & were accommodated in Billets	
ST AUBERT	24		Training &c. Bn moved 2 p.m. to ST AUBERT avoiding shell fire.	
	25		Training &c. Lt Snape goes to 13th Squadron R.A.F. for two days Liaison Course. 2nd Lt. Hallsworth returns from leave.	
CAGNOCLES	26		Bn moved to CAGNOCLES arriving about 14.45 p.m. 2nd Lt Smith returned from leave.	
	27		Church Parades. Training up village & below. 13th Sqdn R.A.F. for 2 day trench course. Rest of Bn. watch 7 Field Performances in a large barn. Capt A.H. Buck rejoins Bn. from course. 2/Lt R.T. Smith goes to 2/Lt Stough returned 2/Lt Latter going also. Reinforcements by acceptance	
	28		Training &c. Troops to 5 events required	
	29		Training &c. officers attend 9th Cheshire officers' flying course	
	30		Major Mosten goes to Hospital. 2/Lt Lotens retains from course.	
	31		Bn scheme Bn brake 9 & 6 Division command	
			Bn carried on. Brigade Scheme	

J.W. Sadreyne Lieut Colonel
Commanding Bn (8) Batt Hunts Cyclist Regt.

8th (S) Batt. North Stafford. Regt.

Army Form C. 2118.

WAR DIARY

INTELLIGENCE SUMMARY.

(Erase heading not required.)

For NOVEMBER 1918

Instructions regarding War Diaries and Intelligence Summaries are contained in F. S. Regs., Part II. and the Staff Manual respectively. Title pages will be prepared in manuscript.

Place	Date 1918	Hour	Summary of Events and Information	Remarks and references to Appendices
CAGNOLLET	Nov.1		Battalion moved by march route to WILLERVAL in 3 hours and then entraining to sidings near MONCHY-LE-PREUX. Went on leaving train to bivouac area near CAGNOLLET.	
VENDIGNIES AU MERCHER	2		Bn marched into support line and being about 1000 yds N.W. of MAISIÈRES. Enemy shelled in the Bn with W. of MAISIÈRES area with main Bull in VENDIGNIES au MERCHER.	
	3		On orders Battalion advanced to a position 2000 yds N.E. of MAISIÈRES the night being dark and wet. FME DE WAULT.	
	4		05.30 hours Battalion by keeping direction with compass through TERRAIN Enemy shelled this village very heavily with gas. Bn. deployed on Brigade Frontage of 58 Brigade were on right. Enemy Machine (Guns) (Points) N.E. WARGNIES LE GRAND) and Snipers offered stiff opposition but with support of WM.G. WARGNIES LE GRAND North Staffs 1st B. C. in front of W.B. & Other Ranks Battalion high ground 1300 yds N.E. Bn. captured. Our casualties & WM G. Wright and 2 Lieut J. Chapple were and other ranks 14 killed, 98 and 1 wounded. Enemy Sergt. surrendered, other ranks twenty negative. 1 M.G. Gun an enemy a few guns & Camelier possibly offered strong resistance [?].	

WAR DIARY FOR NOVEMBER 1918
or
INTELLIGENCE SUMMARY

Army Form C. 2118.

8th (S) Batt. North Stafford Regt.

Instructions regarding War Diaries and Intelligence Summaries are contained in F. S. Regs., Part II. and the Staff Manual respectively. Title pages will be prepared in manuscript.

(Erase heading not required.)

Place	Date 1918	Hour	Summary of Events and Information	Remarks and references to Appendices
WARGNIES LE GRAND	Nov 4	16.30 hrs	"A" & "D" Coys moved through D.H.Q.'s Coys, under Barrage onto road or 600 yds East of H Ruelin. WARGNIES LE GRAND – B/xy Road on West. Corps line threatened machine gun & rifle fire through their. Shelters gained about ridge 100 yds W. of TIEFNBERIE. Bn moved up in Brigade Con 2.0 Yard (approx) 77 Watt 177 Wallace (3rd in Com.) opposition in TIEFNBERIE slight, scattered MG nests with detachments. E. of HOSIER V Ridge B & C Coys opened heavy artillery and M.G. fire on Enemy retiring artillery. Bn got excellent targets, appears unable to get away. Front unlimited. Light shells on front.	
LA FLAMENGRIE	6		Low clouds were very trying. Bn dug in with Boundaries on W.E. & S.E. of TIEFNERIE and B.H.Q. to go forward to meet the Bn were relieved by 6/South Staffs Regt. Relief at 02.30 hrs. Bn moved back to ETH arriving about 05.30 hrs. Bn feeding, dried now. La FLAMENGRIE.	
ETH.	7		Bn moved off at 09.00 to LA FLAMENGRIE. 2/Lieut. Jerram Joins on leave Later 2/Lieut. Jerram received further orders arriving about Snowing.	
LA FLAMENGRIE	8		from TRISNIERS arrived there. Message was not shelled.	

8th (S) Batt. North Stafford. Regt.

WAR DIARY for NOVEMBER 1918

INTELLIGENCE SUMMARY

Army Form C. 2118.

Place	Date	Hour	Summary of Events and Information	Remarks and references to Appendices
TAISNIERES BRY	Nov. 9		Bn. remained here until morning of 10th when it moved to BRY.	
	10		Arriving at 13.30 hrs.	
	11		News received at 09.30 hrs. that hostilities will cease at 11.00 hrs. Troops to stand fast in their present position. Defensive precautions will be taken and no intercourse of any kind with the enemy.	
	12		Bn. cleaning up and clearing billets, arranging for Lns. Hunter pass to Hagnies.	
	13		C.O. inspection by Companies. Bn. cleaning up stores & salvaging. 2Lieut. Macken on 1st leave. Warning order received for move of 56th Brigade to VENDIGNIES.	
VENDIGNIES	14		Bn. moved by march route to VENDIGNIES arriving at 14.45 hrs. and were accommodated in billets.	
RIEUX	15		Bn. moved by march route to RIEUX arriving about 12.45 hrs.	
	16		Bn. cleaning up. Bn. paraded at 11.30 hrs. and were addressed by C.O. on the present situation.	
	17		Church parade. The following officers joined the Bn. Hunts & H/Johnson, H/Jones, S.E. Ward, V. Nathan H. Howlett, R.D. Hancock. Capt R.B. Bainbridge M.C. from to Brigade H.Qrs.	
	18		Lieut F.J. Cotts rejoined and Lieut. Sadler, Forte & Broadhurst joined.	

8th (S) Batt. North Stafford. Regt.   Army Form C. 2118.

WAR DIARY
INTELLIGENCE SUMMARY.
(Erase heading not required.)

FOR NOVEMBER 1918

Place	Date 1918	Hour	Summary of Events and Information	Remarks and references to Appendices
RIEUX	Nov. 19		Training.	
	20		do.	
	21		Training & Salvaging. Lieut Glynn Jones. Visit of Divisional Follies.	
	22		Training & Salvaging. Warning order received for move to CAMBRAI.	
	23		BEAVOURNE area. 2/Lieut Lyford reported from Leave. Lieut Alcock reported from Reserve.	
			Training & Salvaging.	
			2/Lieut W. Wilson & 1/0r. & 7/0 R. joined.	
	24		Church parade. Baths &c.	
	25		Bn. moved by route march to CAMBRAI arriving about 13:55 hrs. and were accommodated in billets.	
CAMBRAI	26		Training.	
	27		do. Lieut F. Smith joined. 2/Lieut Jervois reported from Leave.	
	28		do. Drafts of 3 Officers (Lieut Forrest, & Lieuts Foster & Warren S/Henson) and 100 Other ranks joined Bn.	
TALMAS	29		Bn. march by lorry to TALMAS the day being very wet.	
	30		General cleaning up of billets.	

H. Sabery Lieut Colonel
Commanding 8th (S.) Batt. North Stafford. Regt.

8TH (SERVICE) BATTALION NORTH STAFFORDSHIRE REGIMENT.

An account of operations from Nov. 2nd. to Nov. 9th.

2nd. Battalion left VRIGNES and partly relieved elements of 61st
Division W. of MURIGNIES and dug in. Night cold but fine.

3rd. On forward Battalions advancing to W outskirts of JENLAIN
Battalion at 0530 moved to a position 2000 N.W. MURIGNIES
where it dug in. The night very dark and very wet. (Battalion
H.Q. at Fme. de GAULT.)

4th. At 5.40 Battalion advanced so as to cross Blue Line at 0620.
Owing to thick mist progress slower than expected, although
excellent direction on the whole was kept. Blue Line was
crossed about 0630 and directly afterwards the enemy barrage was
met. At this time the enemy was heavily shelling the village
outskirts and river with Gas and H.E. and it was necessary to adjust
Gas Masks. I am glad to be able to add another Commanding Officer's
voluntary testimony for the steadiness with which the Companies
went through the barrage. A number of casualties were suffered before
reaching Green Line, including 4 Officers. En Route through the
village one Company mopped up a German Machine Post and 8 prisoners.
Battalion H.Q. went through N. of Village and arrived at Green Line
slightly in advance of Companies who were delayed at the River.

(b). With exception of two Platoons of a leading Company, all
Coys. had accurately located themselves, and went forward through the
Cheshires, to take Red Line; Support Company temporarily lending two
Platoons to a leading Company. and
The advance to Red Line was some 25 minutes late as the protective
barrage had ceased, and the Battalion had to go forward without
any Artillery protection at all. Almost immediately very heavy
Machine Gun Fire was met from the Red Line, and in a short time
close "Pip Squeak" Fire from a Battery just behind BRY. In spite
of this the leading Coys. pushed on in admirable fashion by rushes
as far as the ridge 250 yards E. of Track to BRY, in C.15.a. covering
each other by Lewis Gun and Rifle Fire. There was no cover of any
description. Going over the ground afterwards I counted 7 M.G.
position close to WARGNIES-LE-GRAND - BRY Road, alone, each
with a large pile of empty cases. Two Platoons under Lieut. Harris
attempted to work round the left flank through BRY but were driven
back with a number of Casualties. The 58th Brigade were not up on
the left, there being a gap of about 600 yards in depth. One platoon
tried to work through WARGNIES-LE-GRAND on the right, but were unable
to do so owing to Machine Gun Fire from the hill and wood in C.22.a.
The 24th Division were held up on the river in C.20.d. and a defensive
flank was formed towards WARGNIES-LE-GRAND.
Since leaving the Green Line up to this point, the Battalion had over
100 Casualties including two Officers killed and two wounded.
I got forward a section of Vickers Guns, but could not find the
Advanced Field Guns, who were unable to cross the river till later.
The Coys. dug in, and I asked for Artillery support, without which,
until the 24th Division came up, I saw it would be impossible to advance.
The effects of the Gas through which the men had passed earlier in
JENLAIN was beginning to effect some of the Officers and N.C.O.s
who had been compelled to take off their masks from time to time.
At 1530 orders were received that the advance would continue under
a barrage as far as WARGNIES-LE-GRAND - BRY Road. I sent through
the Support and Reserve Coys. who gained their objectives without
difficulties and with few casualties, including Captain A.W.BIRCH.
The enemy evidently retiring as soon as barrage was opened.
Night quiet and fine.

5th At 0600 K.S.L.I. went through under a barrage and later Battalion went forward and continued the advance on their left, as far as East outskirts of LA FLAMENGRIE. Casualties Capt. & Adjt. E.C.GOOD and the Rev. T.J.WALLACE and a few Other Ranks. At 1640 enemy put down a heavy barrage of all calibres and Machine Guns in H.7.c. and d. and 13.a. and b. Owing to this, the darkness and heavy rain it was not possible to reach the Brown Line. Night very wet and cold.

6th At 0600 under a barrage, advance again continued, and with not many casualties, including one Officer, Brown Line was reached.
Two Sections F.A. and 8 Vickers were sent up in Support and gallantly took up exposed positions on the ridge in H.14.b. Very heavy M.G. and Artillery Fire was met on reaching the Brown Line, and the Coys. dug in, in depth, and sent forward patrols to cross the river. Every endeavour was made, but Machine Gunners and Snipers along Railway and in the wood behind made this impossible, although two posts were established on the river, and later in the afternoon a N.C.O. and 6 men of "B" Coy. got across and established a post on the Railway embankment.
Rain fell heavily all day, and the going was very heavy. The men and Officers were by this time almostl completly exhausted and wet through; and rifles and Lewis Guns caked with mud which it was almost impossible to scrape off. Coys. were much reduced in strength, especially in Officers and N.C.O.s, "D" Coy. being commanded by a 2nd. Lieut., lent from another Company while his second in command was a Lance Corporal. The shelling all day was very heavy and never for one minute stopped. Orders to adavnace at 15.30 across the river were, I am thankful to say cancelled at 14.45; as I do not honestly believe in face of the opposition the enemy was then putting up the exhaustion of the men and the condition of their arms, the lateness of the orders, and the extremly difficult and wheeling advance they were called upon to make with very few leaders, that the operation would have had the least chance of success.
Another and important reason was that by this time the Officers' Maps were an unreadable pulp. I lay stress on these points as I do not think that the higher Command can have been aware of the conditions at the time the orders were issued. Personally during the whole operation up to 1800 this day I saw no Staff Officer other than the Brigade Major, who visited me once at about 0900 this day.
The night was very dark and wet.

7th Battalion was relieved by 0400 by the 10th Royal Warwick Regt. and reached ETH about 0600.

8th Battalion moved off 0900 to LA FLEMENGRIE but received further orders to go forward and eventually reached TAISNIERES.,
Arriving there about 17.00 During stay there village was not shelled. Going very heavy across country, rain in afternoon.

9th Battalion remained at this place until the morning of the 10th when it moved to BRY.

WAR DIARY

8th (S). Batt. North Stafford. Regt.

For December 1918

Army Form C. 2118.

Instructions regarding War Diaries and Intelligence Summaries are contained in F. S. Regs., Part II. and the Staff Manual respectively. Title pages will be prepared in manuscript.

INTELLIGENCE SUMMARY
(Erase heading not required.)

Place	Date 1918	Hour	Summary of Events and Information	Remarks and references to Appendices
TANNAY	Dec. 1		Church Parade - Commanding Officer inspection of billets.	
	2		Companies inspected by Commanding Officer - Educational Classes.	
	3		Being a very wet day Battalion had to be cancelled all Companies carried on with work of improving billets. Educational training.	
	4		Training Educational evening.	
	5		do	
	6		Training + Games	Lieut McN Orr rifts 2/N following on leave.
	7		Fen Drill march	
	8		Church Parade 10·0 inspection of A & B Coys Major J. Bell M.C. goes on leave. Lieut H.W. Emerson 2/Lt billets by Rev E.E. Roebeler M.C. joined Battn and posted to "A" Coy.	
	9		On Coys made Educational Games	
	10		Training	
	11		do	
	12		do - A very wet day. Lecture in afternoon by Cpt Stoker.	Lecture on 24/- hr one all alive + on markings for Companies engaged in cleaning billets funeral of your area. Lt W.H. Powis 2/Lt 2/N. Jennings rejoined from Paris leave.
	13			

8th (S) Batt. North Stafford. Regt.   **WAR DIARY** for December 1918.   Army Form C. 2118.

INTELLIGENCE SUMMARY.
(Erase heading not required.)

Instructions regarding War Diaries and Intelligence Summaries are contained in F. S. Regs., Part II. and the Staff Manual respectively. Title pages will be prepared in manuscript.

Place	Date 1918	Hour	Summary of Events and Information	Remarks and references to Appendices
TALMAS	Dec 14		Training & Educational Classes. 2/Lt A.S Mark Gmr to England & further measures for further Men.Tr. in new camp.	
MONTRELET	15		Bn moved by march route to MONTRELET arriving about 15.30 hr. & were accommodated in billets	
	16		Bn moved by march route to VILLERS L'HOPITAL arriving about 15.00 hr. and were accommodated in Holstead Camp.	
			2/Lt L.Farrant reported from Stobbils. The Bn were complimented by the G.O.C. 174th Inf.Bde. on arrival from march from TALMAS Bn carried out Hygienic measures in accord with order issued by 56th Inf. Bde Camp	
	17		Training as Defensive VB.	
	18		Training. Working parties Improvement of Camp.	
	19		10.30 hr. Parade 250 other ranks Temporary Command C.O. & 2/Lt R.S.Mw Kelly	
			C.O. & 2/Lt Market training & Lectures	
	20		Attended Church Service	
			Training Camp Improvement	
	21		Lecture 2/Lt. C. Masters jointed Bn from base. 2/Lt Long left for duty with 2/6th North Staffords	
			Pte G.D. Mark returned from leave 2/Lt J.W. Denis & 2/Lt R. Warwick Rejtl. to Join. 10 x R.Warwicks Reps to join Bn for Temp. duty	
	22		Training. Working parties Improvement of Camp	
	23		Working parties Enclosure and Drainage Improvement of Camp	
			Lieut A.S.A. Erie retd am M.S. 3 French Bn	

Army Form C. 2118.

Instructions regarding War Diaries and Intelligence Summaries are contained in F. S. Regs., Part II. and the Staff Manual respectively. Title pages will be prepared in manuscript.

8th (S) Batt. North Stafford. Regt.

WAR DIARY or INTELLIGENCE SUMMARY.

for December 1918

(Erase heading not required.)

Place	Date 1918	Hour	Summary of Events and Information	Remarks and references to Appendices
VILLERS L'HOPITAL	Dec 24		Nothing. Baths, Education & Gymnastic programme of Camp. Major J.T. [?] M.C reported from leave and took over army command of Battalion. vice Capt. R.W. Leckie.	
	25		Church Parades. Rations issued down at [?] this day. Men had the usual Xmas day and [?] and enjoyed themselves. Men [?] bomb [?] no [?] till [?] the incidence of [?].	
			[illegible handwritten paragraph]	
	26		[illegible handwritten paragraph] Boxing day [?] a general holiday [?] were [?] [?] in the Troops [?] [?].	
	27		[illegible handwritten paragraph]	

Army Form C. 2118.

8th (S) Batt. North Stafford. Regt.

WAR DIARY for December 1918

INTELLIGENCE SUMMARY
(Erase heading not required.)

Instructions regarding War Diaries and Intelligence Summaries are contained in F. S. Regs., Part II. and the Staff Manual respectively. Title pages will be prepared in manuscript.

Place	Date 1918	Hour	Summary of Events and Information	Remarks and references to Appendices
MILLERS L'HOPITAL	Dec 28		Educational training. Horses & 1st & 2nd field days gone on leave.	
	29		A football match between a very large party of officers of the 3rd Bn Worcester Regt. and officers of 8th N. Staffords was played in the afternoon and resulted in a win for 8th Bn. Regt 10 goals to 3	
	30		Working parties. Educational training. Appointment of Camp Instructor. Lt. the Master of Ringsbruck in the General Dir. Q.M. Return 1140 having DEMOBILIZED as awaits at 10. Lt. G.N. Taylor D.S.O. and Lieut (acting) R.H. Queenzeyhting with Liggets Lieut (acting) R.H. Dunscomb went to France and Ld. R.W. Sargeant M.C. mentioned in dispatches and wounded in action.	
	31		Being a wet day Bn. made sunlecto + Coys warmed in myselfice and drill in huts.	

Signed [signature]
Lieut-Colonel,
Commanding 8th (S.) Batt. North Stafford. Regt.

WAR DIARY for JANUARY 1917
8th (S) Bn NORTH STAFFS REGT
INTELLIGENCE SUMMARY

Army Form C. 2118.

Place	Date 1917	Hour	Summary of Events and Information	Remarks and references to Appendices
VILLERS L'HOPITAL	Jan 1		Troops at disposal of O.C. Coys	
	2		Bn parade Drill etc. Formation at Flanks. The morning awards published in Gazette include 2nd Lt Hot Tabuteau D.S.O.	
	3		Bn to D.S.O. Major St Martin D.S.O.	
	4		Bn route march B Coy on Range. Educational classes. Troops paraded to Smith on parade present Flaviende classes. Lt Col St Martin informed troops that Major Knight + 20 Officers Rank 15	
	5		other ranks had been awarded to Smith for forwarding station. Church Parade. Surround (Officers) football competition (Semi Final) 2nd N Staffs v 9th Cha Regt (under 11 Staff 9th Cheshire Regt V.O. two legs working parties International classes	
	6		B Coy on Range. Route march VILLERS L'HOPITAL - BONNIERES - VILLERS L'HOPITAL	
	7		Bn Rehab march	
	8		Educational classes. Battn parade for Drill the international classes Visit of Maj Gen T.A. Cubitt. Marche of 5th W. D. Bn.	
	9		Bn parade for Drill firing on Range 2nd R Batt goes on leave	
	10		Train parade to Bn + 2nd N Staff Relt. Bn parade for Drill firing on Range Educational classes working parties to 1st Btn on move Bn parade + Musketry classes. Fathr Letuijnes.	
	11		Bn parade for Drill etc International classes Gotta Tournament (officers) 5th W. D. Bn wins by 4 goals to Nil. Final of 2nd + 9th Staffs Regt v 2nd W.D. Bn. Ranks to surprise leave for demob etc.	
	12		5th W. D. won by 4 goals to 1 goal of Cheshire Regt.	
	13		12 Other Ranks to disposal Front on 10 O.R.s to disposal Fort for educ Church parade D.J.H. Divning on Range 1 Officer + 5 O.R.s paraded to Cross Bn parade for Drill. D.J. Living n. Range 170.R. 5 Other Ranks for Cambridge in Station n Range Battn demonstration School Gotta Studies + 29	
	14		Bn parade for Drill working parties International classes (Officers + Other Ranks + the Final Camp for demobilization. In the evening the officers were	

Army Form C. 2118.

8th (S) Bn. York & Lanc Regt. WAR DIARY JANUARY 1919. Cont.
or
INTELLIGENCE SUMMARY.
(Erase heading not required.)

Place	Date 1919	Hour	Summary of Events and Information	Remarks and references to Appendices
VILLERS L'HOPITAL	Jan 14		a carnival which opened a great success. the Bn Band had played and was present together with officers from the units of the Brigade	
	15		Troops turned out full. Rehearsal for Guard party & General to-morrow. Inspection of Games.	
	16		Bn had an inspection of Inventions & Arms. Educational classes.	
	17		Bn Route March. Educational classes.	
	18		Bn Foot ball. Educational classes. 12 other ranks proceeded to dispersal camp & out sentry men.	
	19		French funeral. Draft of NCOs & Men 1915 - 13 other Ranks authorised. Officers Rugby match. Bn interior econ & employment.	
	20		Capt R.W. Owen N.C. goes on leave. Lt Hy on range scheme. Capt R.W. Allen 2/4 Y.R Rifles acting in other Unit. educational classes to disperse camp. the histology film. Capt W. Wilson, Inspection.	
	21		Proceeded to dispersal camp. Demobilization commenced owing to Educational Classes. Bn parade in rehearsal of presentation of colours. Educational classes. Lt ? walked ... 2/Lt ... H.J. Hall and the Other Ranks to dispersal camp	
	22		for demobilization. Parade for full Turnout. Gen S.W. Hammond G.O.C. attended the DAM. 22 Other Ranks 60 Inverness Regt. for Disper'l.	
	23		10 TT dogs handed for Full. B. gt on range. Rifle fire in from 200 m Proceeded down to range dynamized in town rapidly.	
	24		Bn route march.	

Instructions regarding War Diaries and Intelligence Summaries are contained in F. S. Regs., Part II. and the Staff Manual respectively. Title pages will be prepared in manuscript.

8th (S) Bn North Staffs Regt — **WAR DIARY** *or* **INTELLIGENCE SUMMARY.** (*Erase heading not required.*) — JANUARY 1919 Contd.

Army Form C. 2118.

Place	Date 1919	Hour	Summary of Events and Information	Remarks and references to Appendices
VILLERS L'HOPITAL	JAN. 24		Lieut E. Roberts M.M. takes over duty of Adjutant.	
	25		Bn parade for Drill less C Coy. Educational Classes. Baths. 2/Lt E.C. Weaver & 23 Other Ranks to dispersal camp for demobilization.	
	26		Church parades. Lieut R.D. Hancock & 24 Other Ranks to dispersal camp for demobilization.	
	27		Rehearsal for Colour party & Escort. C Coy on Range. A B & D Coys at disposal of Coys. Educational Classes. Lt A.J. Ellington and 24 O.Rs to dispersal camp for demobilization.	
	28		Bn parade for rehearsal of presentation of Colours. Educational Classes. 2/Lt S.H. Machin and 24 O Ranks to dispersal camp for demobilization.	
	29		Bn route march. Educational Classes. 13 Other Ranks to dispersal camp for demobilization. The following awards to Officers & O.Rs by H.M. the King in connection with New Year honours dispatch. Bar to D.S.O. Lieut Col. H.W. Dakeyne D.S.O. D.S.O. Major L.E. Martin M.C. M.S.M. 13925 C.S.M. Alcock H. 52371 C.S.M. Darby J.H. 17863 R.Q.M.S. Scott J. 40785 Pte Bell H.	
	30		Final rehearsal of presentation & trooping of the Colours. Educational Classes. Lt. F. Smith from Concentration Camp for Demobilization.	
	31		Coys at disposal of O.C. Coys for improvement of Camp. Educational Classes. Baths.	

H. Dakeyne
Lieut. Colonel,
Commanding 8th (S.) Batt. North Stafford. Regt.

D. D. & L., London, E.C. (10340) Wt W5300/P713 750,000 3/18 **E 2688** Forms/C2118/16.

WAR DIARY 8TH N. STAFFORD REGT.
or
INTELLIGENCE SUMMARY.

Army Form C. 2118.

Place	Date	Hour	Summary of Events and Information	Remarks and references to Appendices
Villers L'hopital	FEB. 1919			
	1		Coys at disposal of Os. C. Educational Classes.Baths.11 O.Rs. to Dispersal Cmp for Demob.	
	2		Church Parades.15 O.Rs. to Dispersal Camp for Demob.	
	3		2 coys on the Range, 2coys on fatigues.Educational Classes.12 O.Rs.todispersal camp for demob.	
	4		Coys at Disposal of Os.C.Educational Classes.Lieut C.J.Hunter,M.C. goes on leave.	
	5		Coys at Disposal of OS.C. for cleaning equipment.Educational Classes.Alcture by Col.Montgomery D.S.O. on the "Strategy of 1918" was delivered in the cinema.	
	6		Coys at disposal of Os,.C.Educational Classes .Capt.F.Crewe goes on leave.Cpt E. J.Colls proceeded to BASE DEPOT Calais.LT.G.W.Broadhurst &18 O.Rs. to Dispersal Camp for Demob.	
	7		Coys at Disposal of Os.C. for cleaning equipment.Retreat at 1700Hrs.from G.Hav.Baths. 11O.Rs. to Dispersal Camp for Demob. Followed by the good-bye from Maj-Gen.G.D.J.ff, G.B. C.M.G. C- of 19th Division. "On the occasion of his leaving the 19th Division to take command of the 30th Division,Maj-Gen.Jeffreys bids farewell to all those who have served under him &wishes them whether in the Army or in Civil life ,the best of good luck & happiness. The Division has at all times lived up to the highest standard of the British Army,& its units have been conspicuous alike for there fine spirit in action,&for there good conduct & discipline behind the line. The Maj-Gen parts with them with the greatest regret;he thanks them for all they have done in the past; & he feels sure that they will matain to the end the good name of the division & the high standard of honour & duty for which it has always been distinguished. (presentation & 6th rehearsal of the trooping of the Colour.Educational Classes .Visit of Divisional Follies.	
	8		Church Parades.	
	9		Consecration & Presentation of the Colours. Consecrated by Richt.Rev. Bishop Gwynne,Lord Bishop of Khartoum,& Presented by (Capt.) H.R.H. The Prince of Wales K.G.,M.C., The batt. paraded (as part of the 56 BDE)on the Bde Parade ground in readiness for the ceremony. The Colours of the 9th Cheshire regiment & 8th North Staffs.Regt.were unfurled by the 2nds. in Command & Consecrated by the Acting Chaplain General,Bishop Gwynne. They were then handed by the 2nds. in Command, to the Prince who presented them to 2/Lt.Bass,(9th Cheshire Regt) & Lieut.W.H.Press,(8th Nth.Stafford Regt.) who received them on bended knee; the Colour bearers then rose turned about&faced their Batts.& the Prince made the following speech:-(see att one)	
	10		The ceremony ended with the March Past & Advance in Review order. The steadiness of the men a d the manner in which they marched elicited the praise of all the officers who were privileged	

Army Form C. 2118.

WAR DIARY 8th N. STAFFORD REGT
or
INTELLIGENCE SUMMARY.

(Erase heading not required.)

Instructions regarding War Diaries and Intelligence Summaries are contained in F. S. Regs., Part II. and the Staff Manual respectively. Title pages will be prepared in manuscript.

Place	Date	Hour	Summary of Events and Information	Remarks and references to Appendices
Villers L'Hopital	Feb. 1919			
	11		Batt. parade for route march.(less "D" Coy)Educational Classes. 120.Rs. to Dispersal Camp for Demob.	
	12		Fatigues. Educational Classes.	
	13		"B" & "D" coys on Range,"A" & "C" fatigues, Education Classes. Capt A.H.Bainbridge M.C. Rejoins from Bde. Hrs.	
	14		Coys at Disposal of Og. C. Educational Classes. 23 O.Rs. to dispersal Camp for Demob. Owing to reduced strength of batt. due to demobilisation companies are finally amalgamated as follows "A" & "D" forming No. 1 coy with Capt B.S. Hancock in command, "B" & "C" forming No.2 coy with Capt. J.A. Riddle in command. Capt R.W.Owen M.C. to hospital sick.	
	15		Coys at disposal of O.C. 50 O.Rs. sent to E.R.C. Hestin. 25 O.RS. to dispersal camp for Demob.	
	16		Church Parades .Capt. J.A.Riddle taken on strength from 8th Gloucester Regt. Cpt A.H. Bainbridge goes on Dispersal draft conducting duty. 25 O.Rs. to dispersal camp for demob.	
	17		Coys at disposal of O.C. for improvement of camp .Educational Classes.Capt. Stoneman goes on leave	
	18		Batt. on fatigue duties.	
	19		Batt. parade to clean up camp & prepare accomodation for 58 Bde.	
	20		Batt. parade to clean up camp	
	21		Coys at Disposal of Os.C. 6 O.Rs. to dispersal camp for demob 2/Lt Kent Draft conducting officer	
	22		Fatigues. Lieut C.J.Hunter rejoined from leave.	
	23		Church Parades.Arrival of part of 58 Bde. Capt R.W.Owen M.C. rejoined from hospital.	
	24		Batt.on fatigue.Remainder of 58 Bde arrive.Capt Crewe rejoined from leave.	
	25		Coys at disposal of Os. C. Lieut C.Roberts M.M. goes on leave.	
	26		Batt. parade for woodcutting.	
	27		Batt on fatigue.	
	28		Lieut Sutherland goes on leave. 8 O.Rs. to dispersal camp for demob.2/Lt W.Warren O.C. DRaft conducting.	

H.S. Osborne
Commanding 8th (S) Bn N. Staffs

Army Form C. 2118.

WAR DIARY
or
INTELLIGENCE SUMMARY.
(Erase heading not required.)

G.H. Staff R.
March 1919
Vol 45

Instructions regarding War Diaries and Intelligence Summaries are contained in F. S. Regs., Part II and the Staff Manual respectively. Title pages will be prepared in manuscript.

Place	Date	Hour	Summary of Events and Information	Remarks and references to Appendices
Villers L' Hopital	March			
	1.		Battalion on fatigue. Lieut. Forrest R.A. returned from Siege Park.	
	2.		Church Parade. Commencing of "Summer Time". 2/Lieut. E.M. Channings goes on Leave.	
	3.		Fatigue duty. Lieut. W.E. Cowlishaw M.C. goes on Leave.	
	4.		Battalion on fatigue.	
	5.		Fatigue duty tarring all huts. Capt. in A.M. Stoneman M.C. rejoins from Leave.	
	6.		Tarring of huts continued. Medical equipment taken on charge of Battn.	
	7.		Fatigues. 5.O.R's to disposal camp for demob. 2/Lieut. Marsh goes draft conducting.	
	8.		Battalion on fatigue.	
	9.		Church Parades. Bn. Football Team played A.S.C. Team at Prevent. Captain A.E. Gore rejoined. From course at 3rd. Army. 2/Lieut. O.C. Sharpe M.C. goes on Leave.	
	10.		Battalion on fatigue duties. Orders received that all Mob. Stores not in use are to be stored at Camiers ready for entraining.	
	11.		Battalion on fatigues.	
	12.		Fatigue duties. Captain J.A. Riddle M.O. goes on Leave. 1 Officer and 10 O.R's of 9th. Cheshire Regt. left to rejoin their unit.	
	13.		Battalion on fatigue.	
	14.		Fatigues. Lieut. H.W. Dakeyne D.S.O. Captain B.S. Hancock & Lieut. E.T. Jacks go on Leave.	
	15.		Lieut. C. Roberts M.M. returned from Leave. 2/Lieut. Williams draft conducting duty 1 man for demob.	
	16.		Battalion parade for wood-cutting.	
	17.		Church Parades. Lieut. T.H. Hallworth M.C. rejoined from course. 2/Lieut. F. Kent returned from Leave.	
	18.		Captain A.E. Gore goes on Leave. Lieut. W.H. Press proceeds to England for duty with 2nd. Bn. North Staffs.	
	19.		Battalion parade for wood-cutting. Lieut H. Sutherland rejoins from Leave.	
	20.		Wood-cutting fatigue. 2/Lieut E.M. Channings returns from draft conducting duty.	
	21.		Fatigue duties. Lieut. M.C. Cowlishaw M.C. rejoins from Leave. Tarring of huts continued. 2.O.R's & 5.Att.O.R's to disposal camp for demob.	

Army Form C. 2118.

WAR DIARY
or
INTELLIGENCE SUMMARY.

(Erase heading not required.)

Instructions regarding War Diaries and Intelligence
Summaries are contained in F. S. Regs., Part II.
and the Staff Manual respectively. Title pages
will be prepared in manuscript.

Place	Date	Hour	Summary of Events and Information	Remarks and references to Appendices
Villers L' Hopital.	March 22.		Marking huts. 7 Officers to dispersal camp for demob. 2/Lieut. W.Warren rejoined from draft conducting duty	
	23.		Church Parade.	
	24.		Fatigues duties.	
	25.		Cleaning up the camp.	
	26.		Marking of huts continued. 2/Lieut. C.G.Simons M.C. returned from Leave Miss L.Ashwell's concert party gave a performance in the cinema at 1800 hours.	
	27.		Fatigues duties. Baths.	
	28.		Fatigue duties.	
	29.		Marking of huts continued.	
	30.		Church Parade.	
	31.		Draft of 2 Officers and 80 O.R's proceeded to 72 Prisoners of War Coy. Dunkirk.	

Bell Major
Lieut Colonel,
Commanding 8th (S) Battn. North Stafford. Regt.

Army Form C. 2118.

WAR DIARY
or
INTELLIGENCE SUMMARY.
(Erase heading not required.)

May 1919.

8th N. Stafford Regt.

Instructions regarding War Diaries and Intelligence Summaries are contained in F. S. Regs., Part II. and the Staff Manual respectively. Title pages will be prepared in manuscript.

Place	Date	Hour	Summary of Events and Information	Remarks and references to Appendices
VILLERS L'HOPITAL	1-5-19		Battalion fatigues etc. Working Party on Rifle Range.	
"	2-5-19		do.	
"	3-5-19		do.	
"	4-5-19		Church Parade.	
"	5-5-19		Battalion fatigues. Working Party renovating Rifle Range.	
"	6-5-19		do.	1. Other Rank sent to hospital.
"	7-5-19		do.	
"	8-5-19		do.	
"	9-5-19		do.	
"	10-5-19		Battalion returned to capts established.	8 Other Ranks sent for dispersal.
"	11-5-19		Church Parade. The 19th Divisional Commander inspected the cadres of Units at Villers L'Hopital and bade them farewell.	
"	12-5-19		Battalion fatigues. Working Party on Rifle Range.	
"			do. Work on rifle range continued.	
"	13-5-19		Loading party left for Candas.	
"	14-5-19		Cadre left Villers L'Hopital by Motor Lorry & proceeded to CANDAS Railhead, where they entrained for STAPLES, acc	

WAR DIARY

8th N. Stafford Regt.

Army Form C. 2118.

Place	Date	Hour	Summary of Events and Information	Remarks and references to Appendices
Le Havre	15/5/19		Battalion Cadre arrived. Havre and all Stores & Transport Vehicles were received.	
Harfleur	16/5/19		Cadre proceeded to Harfleur & were inspected and prepared for embarkation. Billeted in No.2 Embarkation Camp. 2 Other ranks admitted to Hospital.	
"	17/5/19		Cadre remained at No.2 Embarkation Camp. 1 Other rank admitted to Hospital.	
"	18/5/19		Loading party sent to Le Havre where Transport Vehicles and Stores were shipped.	
"	19/5/19		Cadre proceeded to Le Havre and embarked for Southampton.	

Strength of Battalion Cadre — Officers 33. Other Ranks.

Lt. Major
Betts, North Staff... Regt.

CONFIDENTIAL.

Officer i/c
   3rd Echelon Details,
      Balfour House,
         Finsbury Pavement,
           LONDON, E.C.

     Attached A.F. C.2118 (War Diary) of 8th Bn. North Staffordshire Regiment, is forwarded to you for safe custody.

Record Section,
British Troops in
France & Flanders.
6th June, 1919.
DID.

                General Officer Commanding,
         British Troops in France & Flanders.

www.ingramcontent.com/pod-product-compliance
Lightning Source LLC
Chambersburg PA
CBHW081447160426
43193CB00013B/2401